Introduction

In any attempt to understand the Sewell Mountain campaign, it is first necessary to explain the military necessities which ultimately brought upon the scene such men as Robert E. Lee for the South and William S. Rosecrans for the North.

The Sewell Mountain range of West Virginia was in 1861, and is yet today, a wild and rugged region. This is an area where soldier and civilian alike quickly learned what a "hardscrabble" truly was. The expression "this unnatural war" could no where be more appropriate than among the vast wilderness of Big and Little Sewell Mountains, an area which encompasses 112.46 square miles. With a peak elevation of approximately 3,375 feet, the Sewell Mountains extend from the southeastern corner of Fayette County, into Greenbrier County, terminating at present-day Rainelle.

Approximately 32 miles northwest of Sewell Mountain, also in Fayette County, is the town of Gauley Bridge. Situated at the eastern end of the great Kanawha Valley, the town is located at the confluence of the Gauley, Kanawha and New rivers. This community became a prized military target in 1861, and remained so throughout the war. Gauley Bridge was the gate through which all important movements from eastern into southwestern Virginia must necessarily pass. It also formed an important link in any chain of posts designed to cover the Ohio Valley from invasion.

During the Sewell Mountain campaign the town of Gauley Bridge was used by Federal forces as a base of operations. Confederate troops under command of Gen. Henry A. Wise had retreated from the area on July 27, 1861, burning the bridge across the Gauley River, from which the community drew it's name. Gen. Jacob D. Cox and 5,000 Union soldiers occupied the town on July 29, 1861.

From Gauley Bridge the James River and Kanawha Turnpike paralleled New River to the east. Another road extended from Gauley River to Summersville, in Nicholas County, a distance of

about 30 miles, with a side road to Cross Lanes and Carnifex Ferry, another strategically important location. From Summersville, this road continued northward to Sutton and Weston, thus making a line of communication between northwest Virginia and the Kanawha Valley. The Giles, Fayette, and Kanawha Turnpike, extended from Kanawha Falls, near Gauley Bridge, through Fayetteville to Flat Top Mountain in Raleigh County, thence to the Narrows of New River, and on to the important Virginia and Tennessee Railroad. Obviously, whoever controlled this region militarily, held a great advantage against their enemy.

Southward from Big Sewell Mountain, at a distance of about 30 miles, lay the little town of Lewisburg, Greenbrier County. This was also a strongly pro-Confederate area and was strategically important as a base of operations for campaigns in trans-Allegheny Virginia, as well as being the gateway to southeastern Virginia and eastern Tennessee.

Although no major battles were fought at Sewell Mountain, the loss of man and material to both sides was great. It was among these rolling hills and deep ravines that many young men of the Blue & Gray first experienced the privations and sacrifices of war. From their baptism of fire to the loss of friends and loved ones, it soon became obvious this was not to be a "quick war" as many on both sides of the Mason-Dixon line had predicted. Unprecedented rainfall spawned devastating disease, while daily skirmishes and bushwhacking rapidly thrust these men and boys into the vortex of sanguinary conflict.

The great campaigns of eastern Virginia eventually cast this and all western Virginia campaigns into obscurity. It is hoped that this work will help remedy that wrong. The blood shed at Sewell Mountain was as precious as that lost on the hallowed fields of Gettysburg, or upon the mountains of Tennessee. Many of the boys in gray who participated in this campaign were fighting over soil which they had grown-up on, or farmed, as this was an area of strong Southern sympathy. Still others came from as far away as Mississippi and Louisiana.

The 17,000 soldiers of the Blue & Gray, who struggled

ROBERT E. LEE

AT SEWELL MOUNTAIN:

The West Virginia Campaign

by Tim McKinney

Where Col. Stockton was the Boniface

During the Sewell Mountain campaign the Aaron Stockton residence near Gauley Bridge was Federal Quartermaster Depot. It is today the Glen Ferris Inn.

PICTORIAL HISTORIES PUBLISHING CO., INC.
CHARLESTON, WEST VIRGINIA

LIBRARY OF CONGRESS
CATALOG CARD NUMBER 90-63107

ISBN 0-929521-72-2

First Printing   November 1990
Second Printing March 1993

Typography: Leslie Over
Layout: Stan Cohen
Cover Graphics: Mike Egeler

PICTORIAL HISTORIES PUBLISHING CO., INC.
4103 Virginia Avenue S.E., Charleston, WV 25304

against man and nature in the vast wilderness of Sewell Mountain, deserve recognition. This is their story and, where possible, I have attempted to let the actual participants "speak for themselves" through the use of manuscript and published materials. Writing this story has been, as it always is, an exercise in empathy. I sincerely hope readers will enjoy it, and perhaps, garner some positive lesson from it.

Tim McKinney
June 8, 1990

*This book is dedicated to
my parents.*

Acknowledgments

Without the assistance of numerous institutions and individuals a project such as this would be impossible. The encouragement and contributions of all those listed is truly appreciated. I have attempted to include everyone and I sincerely apologize for anyone I may have accidentally omitted.

The institutions that have provided assistance are: The Ohio Historical Society - Columbus, OH; The Oberlin College Archives - Oberlin, OH; The Rutherford B. Hayes Center - Fremont, OH; The Cincinnati Historical Society - Cincinnati, OH; The Virginia Historical Society - Richmond, VA; The Virginia State Library - Richmond, VA; The Museum of the Confederacy - Richmond, VA; Washington & Lee University - Lexington, VA; Virginia Military Institute Archives - Lexington, VA; West Virginia State Archives - Charleston, WV; West Virginia University - Morgantown, WV; Fayette Co. WV Historical Society - Oak Hill, WV; The Trans Allegheny Historical Association - Beaver, WV; Vining Library - West Virginia Institute of Technology, Montgomery, WV; Tennessee State Archives - Nashville, TN; Georgia State Archives - Atlanta, GA; Mississippi State Archives - Jackson, MS; Louisiana State Archives - Baton Rouge, LA; Wilson Library, University of North Carolina - Chapel Hill, NC; William R. Perkins Library - Durham, NC; U.S. Army Military Historical Institute - Carlisle Barracks, PA; West Point Museum - West Point, NY.

I am indebted to numerous individuals, some of whom I have never met, but have been fortunate enough to receive their kind assistance by mail: John Alderman - Roanoke, VA; Alice Todd Alderson - Alderson, WV; Tom Alderson - Beech Mtn., NC; Linda Allen - Vining Library, WV Tech - Montgomery, WV; Bob and Chris Beckelheimer - Oak Hill, WV; John Chapla - Alexandria, VA; Ed and Nina Clark - Kanawha Falls, WV; Stan Cohen - Pictorial Histories Publishing Co. - Charleston, WV and Missoula,

MT; Roger Delauter - Winchester, VA; Jack & Kay Dickinson - Barboursville, WV; Bonnie Estes - Rainelle, WV; Minnie Hall - Mouth of Wilson, VA; W.H. "Rip" Johnson - Rainelle, WV; Dr. and Mrs. J.M. Laing - Lewisburg, WV; W.T. "Wimpy" Lawrence - Fayetteville, WV; Terry Lowry - Charleston, WV; Floyd McClung - Hugheston, WV; Ron Mink - WV Tech - Montgomery, WV; David Myles - Rainelle, WV; Don & Wilma Pomeroy, WV; Dr. Otis K. Rice - Hugheston, WV; Dr. James I. Robertson Jr. - VPI - Blacksburg, VA; Mike Smith & family - Droop Mtn. State Park - Hillsboro, WV; Richard Spearen - Fayetteville, WV; Frances Swope - Lewisburg, WV; Glen Taylor - Robson, WV; Bill Turner - LaPlata, MD; Carroll Walker - Norfolk, VA; Hal Walls - White Sulphur Springs, WV; Noble Wyatt, Poca, WV; and Jim Spounagle and family - Robson, WV. Also thanks to Mr. Joe Ferrell of St. Albans, WV for his editing assistance.

A special thanks to Bob Beckelheimer, George Bragg and Harold Stinnett, of the Fayette Co. WV Historical Society, for helping me place a plaque at the site of Robert E. Lee's Sewell Mtn. WV camp of 1861. This memorial plaque was dedicated Sept. 24, 1989, with the assistance of our local chapter, United Daughters of the Confederacy, and Camp Garnett of the Sons of Confederate Veterans. Reenactors of the 26th Battalion Virginia Infantry and the 36th Regiment Virginia Infantry were also present and assisted us in honoring our Southern ancestors.

I would also like to thank all my friends and relatives; especially my parents, Jerry and Barbara McKinney of Indianapolis, IN, my brothers Jerry and Mark, and my sister Jane, also of Indiana.

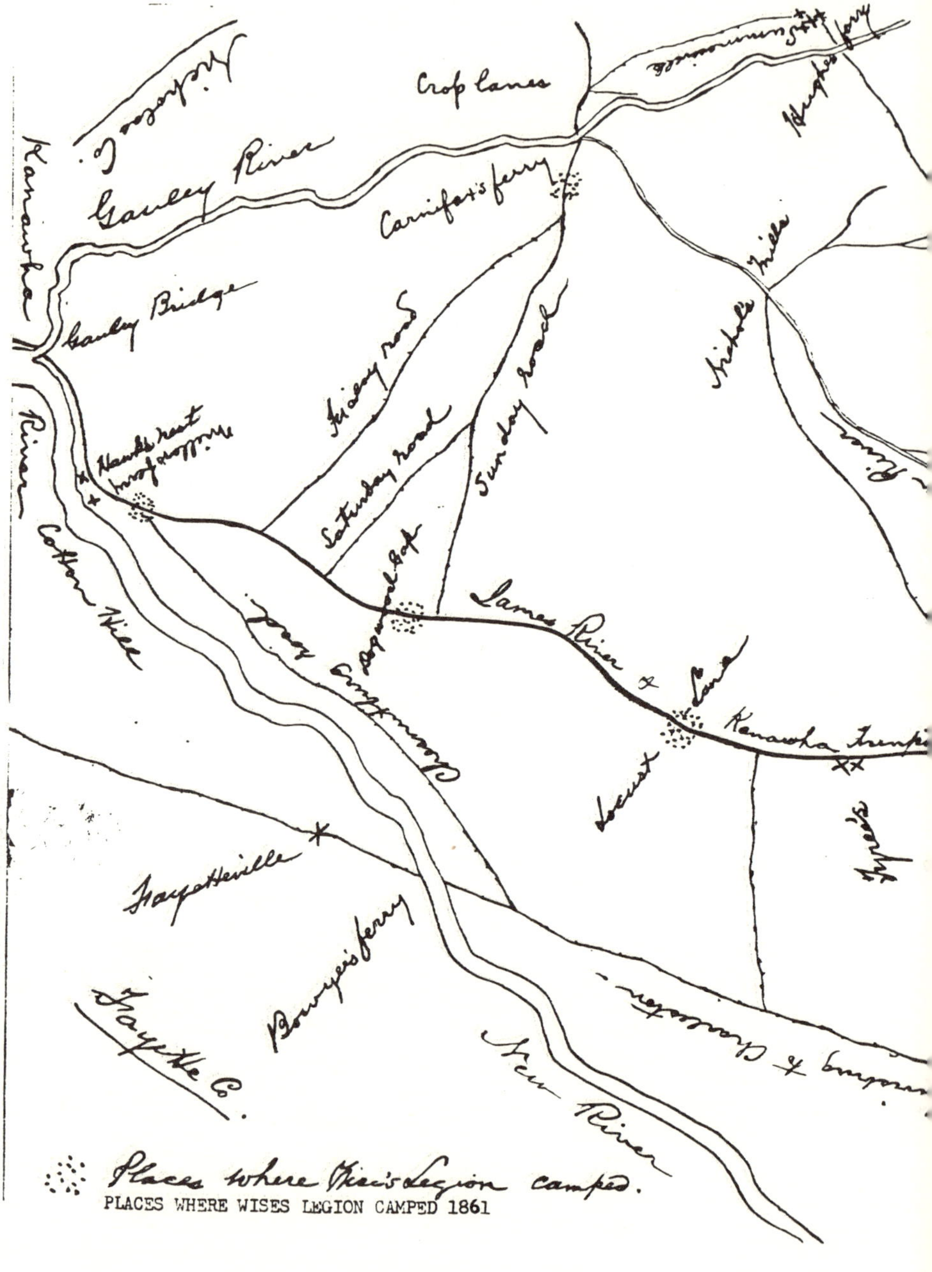

PLACES WHERE WISES LEGION CAMPED 1861

From Lewisburg to Meadow Bluff 16 miles
" " Frazier's 25 "
" " Top of Big Sewell 30 "
" " Locust Lane 39 "
" " Dogwood Gap 48 "
" " Gauley Bridg 62 "
" " Charleston Kanw. 100 "
" " Blue Sulp. Spgs. 13 "
From Charleston to Point Pleasant 57 "
(on the Ohio.)

Mill Creek
Sewell Creek
Greenbrier Co.
Frazier's
Little Sewell Mountain
Meadow River
Meadow Bluff
B.S. + Spring
B.S. Turnpike
Old State Road Fin.
Lewisburg

Gen. John B. Floyd, 1806-1863. A former governor of Virginia and Secretary of War. He commanded the Army of the Kanawha during the Sewell Mountain campaign. COURTESY SWV

Gen. Henry A. Wise, former governor of Virginia. He organized the
Wise Legion in 1861. COURTESY SWV

Table of Contents

First Blood

On Aug. 6, 1861, a meeting was held at White Sulphur Springs, WV, between Confederate Gens. Henry A. Wise and John B. Floyd. Wise and Floyd were both former governors of Virginia, and as rival politicians had developed a hatred for each other which they brought with them into the war. Both men were "political generals" having virtually no military experience. By virtue of his earlier commission General Floyd was senior to Wise and thus entitled to command their combined forces when they were operating together.[1]

Their meeting at the White Sulphur was anything but amiable. General Wise was known for long "windbag" speeches and he exercised his talents considerably in explaining his retreat from the Kanawha Valley, 70 miles northwest of White Sulphur Springs.[2] This retreat, completed on July 31, did not meet with the approval of Floyd and he wasted no time informing Wise of his desire to retake the Kanawha Valley. Wise was firmly against the move, saying it would take at least two weeks to refit his command and obtain the wagons needed for an advance.[3]

Despite Wise's objections, Floyd informed him on August 8 that he was anxious to begin a move toward the Kanawha Valley, and he asked Wise for a detailed list of the forces Wise had available for duty. In his response we can see how Wise earned his reputation as a "unique character and master quarreler."[4] He stated that at no time had his men been supplied with sufficient clothing, camp equipage, arms, tents, shoes, and other needs. Wise also complained that 300 of his men were in the hospital.[5] Actually, General Floyd's command was in no better condition, and fully half of his men were sick with measles.[6]

On Aug. 10, Wise wrote a letter to Gen. Robert E. Lee, who was then camped at Valley Mountain, in Pocahontas County.[7] Among other things, Wise asked if he might be sent some weapons that had been taken from the Yankees at Manassas. He had written to Lee previous to that in an unsuccessful attempt to have his command permanently separated from that of Floyd.[8]

The next day, Aug. 11, Floyd assumed total command of all Confederate forces intended to operate against the Yankees in the Kanawha Valley and adjacent country. This order did not sit well with Wise, and there began what was to become a death blow to Confederate efforts in southern West Virginia generally.[9] General Wise wanted to draw the Union army into the eastern wilderness of Fayette County, at Sewell Mountain. He argued that to advance all the way to the Kanawha River, 32 miles northwest of the Sewell Mountains, and 62 miles northwest of Lewisburg, would require their army to haul supplies an additional 30 miles over some of the worst roads in western Virginia. Despite Wise's plan, Floyd wanted to advance into the Kanawha Valley and drive back the Federal troops then occupying the valley, commanded by Gen. Jacob D. Cox. General Lee was able to temporarily settle the matter by choosing Wise's plan as the best.[10]

On Aug. 13, Wise again wrote to Lee in another attempt to separate his command from Floyd's, and he asked that Floyd's orders to his brigade be communicated through him. Lee responded that he felt no orders were necessary on the subject, and attempted to pacify Wise's ego: "I hope," he wrote, "I need not assure you that I never entertained the least doubt as to your zealous and cordial cooperation in every effort against the common enemy. Your whole life guarantees the belief that your every thought and act will be devoted to the sacred cause, dearer than life itself, of defending the honor and integrity of the State."[11]

Unfortunately, cordial cooperation would never occur between Wise and Floyd. As events leading up to the Sewell Mountain campaign unfolded the aggregate Confederate forces available in the region exceeded 6,000 troops. This includes the Virginia militia forces of Gens. Alfred Beckley and Augustus A. Chapman, recently organized and designated the 27th and 19th Brigades respectively. Federal forces in the region totaled approximately 5,000 including cavalry and artillery. Their headquarters had been established at Gauley Bridge.

General Floyd moved the 1,800 men under his command to Meadow Bluff, Greenbrier County, and on Aug. 14, after growing impatient with the delaying tactics of Wise, peremptorily ordered him to march with his brigade of approximately 2,000 men and join him at Meadow Bluff.[12] Wise complied with this order on Aug. 15, after writing a letter of complaint to General Lee, advising him of the situation and offering his opinions as to the best course of action.[13]

As Wise was on the march, General Floyd sent a scouting party to Sewell Mountain, and began moving his entire command to that point. The scouts, commanded by Col. Henry Heth and Col. James L. Davis, advanced over the rough and muddy turnpike a distance of 17 miles. Upon reaching the western foot of Big Sewell Mountain, Floyd's unsuspecting scouts clashed with a 120-man scouting party from the 11th Ohio Infantry, commanded by Col. Joseph W. Frizell.

Earlier in the day Frizell and his men had left their post at Gauley Bridge with the stated purpose of finding the enemy. Their ride had taken them over 30 miles through rough and broken country with only an occasional home or mountain tavern encountered. This was the furthest any organized Federal force had penetrated into southwest Virginia, and Frizell's men were anxious for the fight. As they rode along the winding turnpike and began their approach to the western foot of Big Sewell Mountain, Lt. John D. Shannon of the 11th Ohio, Company B, observed the Rebel cavalry advancing a short distance ahead. Shannon was in command of the advance guard and as such had only a few men with him. He knew he could not risk an engagement with the enemy until the others had come up. Acting quickly, Shannon ordered his men off into the thickets which lined the left side of the road. He then ordered a private to hold their horses and notify the others of the impending fight. Shannon continued his advance on foot, crouching in the thickets for cover and using hand signals to control the movements of his men. While searching for the best position from which to ambush the Rebels, a member of the Confederate advance guard caught sight of the Yankees and opened fire.

Suddenly the entire scene was one of chaos and smoke. Almost immediately, two men of Company B, 11th Ohio, were wounded. Pvt. Will Rae was crouched in the brush with a bullet through his right hand, while Pvt. Augustus Houck suffered a similar injury to his left hand. The mountains echoed with the sounds of combat and a brisk skirmish was kept up for several minutes before Colonel Frizell and the others were on the scene. Joshua Horton of the 11th Ohio described the event: "Hearing the firing, the colonel gave the order to double-quick, and upon turning a bend in the road a squad of Rebel cavalrymen were encountered, who gave and returned a volley and then retreated. The colonel formed an ambush and sent out scouts from Company H, under Lieutenant Weller, who also encountered Rebels and received and returned a fire. After waiting for some time and no enemy appearing in the road, it was thought best to fall back...”[14]

Not knowing the strength of the enemy in his front, Colonel Heth ordered his Confederate cavalry to regroup and await developments. Heth's men had suffered two killed and three wounded in the skirmish. Colonel Frizell very much wanted to capture some Rebels and planned an advance for later that evening, but a majority of his officers deemed an immediate retreat advisable. The Yankees already had three men wounded and it was decided the risk was not worth the gain. Accordingly, the Federal forces fell back to their camps at Gauley Bridge and vicinity. The Confederate scouts anxiously waited at the foot of Big Sewell until it was decided to fall back two or three miles from the scene of the skirmish, to the top of the mountain. This movement was completed at nightfall and a camp was established in the moonlight upon the crest of Big Sewell. Here, amid the towering pines and majestic oaks, and under the watchful eye of the hoot owl and whippoorwill, the weary Confederates penned a few letters home by the flickering light of their campfires.

What a day this had been. For many of the participants on both sides this had been their baptism of fire. While it was not a bloody fight of the type they would experience as the war dragged on, it left with them a lasting impression of war and hardship. While this first clash of arms at Sewell was a minor affair, it served as a barometer of events which would transpire in the coming weeks.

Later that same night as the command of General Wise arrived at Meadow Bluff after a tiring march of 24 miles, an incident occurred which severely taxed the patience and energy of several of Wise's officers and men. Addison B. Roler of the Wise Legion described the event: “It was some time of night when we got there but there was moonshine. Just as we were driving into the encampment over the bridge that was built over the creek, owing to the unusual weight that was on our wagons, a five-horse team which was hauling our baggage, knapsacks and all, fell through. The bridge was crushed and down went wagon, horses, driver and all. Fortunately, both sides of the bridge gave way at the same place at the same instant...we unloaded the wagon and was soon encamped for the night, such as it was sleeping on the ground without putting up our tents or eating."[15]

The following day Floyd and Wise arrived in the vicinity of Sewell Mountain, with Wise camping near the eastern foot, in an oat field. The next day, Aug. 17, General Floyd advanced with a portion of his command to the western foot of Sewell Mountain and established headquarters at the fine home of Frank and Margaret Tyree. This house still stands and is known as the Old Stone House, or Tyree Tavern. It is located along the old James River and Kanawha Turnpike, near Ravens Eye. This house was built in 1824 by Richard Tyree, who had moved to Fayette County from Richmond in 1816. Used as a stagecoach stop and inn, the house became a prized possession by the commanders of troops operating in the vicinity.[16]

Frank and Margaret Tyree were Confederate in sympathy and their two sons had enlisted in the Southern army. Frank occasionally volunteered as a Rebel scout and Mrs. Tyree was rumored to be a Confederate spy. The loyalty and friendship of the Tyree family made a lasting impression on Joseph A. Brown of the 22nd Virginia Infantry: "At the foot of Little Sewell on the west, pioneer Frank Tyree and his wife and children lived, influential Presbyterians, and were noted among the mountain dwellers. Mrs. Tyree was a remarkable woman--fearless as any stalwart of either company and decidedly defiant. It was said that she stood in her chicken house with an axe in her hand and defended it from marauding Federal soldiers. It was commonly known among the Dixie boys that in the darkness of night she managed to reach General Lee, riding miles alone through the mountains, and had given Lee valuable information."[17]

Prior to Floyd's advance to Tyree's, he wrote a letter to Confederate President Jefferson Davis complaining about Wise's earlier retreat from the Kanawha Valley and about his defiant attitude. Floyd suggested that the Wise Legion be replaced with troops from Kentucky: "I have taken command formally, but his unwillingness to cooperate...is so great that it amounts practically almost to open opposition. I know very well how to enforce obedience, and will, without the least hesitation, do it. There is no danger of a rupture between us, I think, but it would be far better to observe a cordial cooperation amongst commands in the Kanawha Valley. Wise would serve zealously and cheerfully under General Lee, and more so with anyone than with me...The force to replace Wise should, if possible, come from Kentucky."[18]

Floyd was mistaken in his statement that there would be no rupture between himself and Wise. There had been a rupture from the first day their commands were designated to operate together. At no time before, during, or after the Sewell Mountain campaign, did these political generals operate harmoniously.

As Floyd's headquarters were established at Tyree's, he sent an order to General Wise directing him to occupy the top of Big Sewell Mountain and there to await further orders. Wise grudgingly complied with this order and quickly established picket and rear guard positions while studying the topography of the site with a view towards its defense.[19] The following day he penned a long rambling letter to General Lee, enclosing copies of all the correspondence between himself and Floyd relevant to the distinction of the Wise Legion as a separate and independent entity from the army of General Floyd: "My officers of the Legion cannot be permitted to disregard my general orders nor to take orders directly from General Floyd, and I shall utterly disregard it...I lay the case before you in time to prevent collision. My regiments are reduced by measles 50 per cent, and the cavalry are ruined; nothing but hay, and no shoes."[20]

Also on Aug. 18, Floyd notified Wise that he had moved his headquarters from Tyree's to the western top of Sewell Mountain, a position about one mile away from, and within sight of, the Wise Legion camp. He explained that this move was made as the latter position was more defensible. Soon a cold rain began which would continue for two days, adding considerably to the discomfort of the troops.[21]

On Aug. 19, General Floyd sent marching orders to Wise: "Brig. Gen. Henry A. Wise will take up the line of march tomorrow at 7:30 a.m., and proceed with all the forces under his command in the direction of the Kanawha Valley, by way of the James River and Kanawha Turnpike. He will place for the march, his artillery next to his advance guard of cavalry, and his horse in the rear of his column."[22]

Wise was delayed on the 20th in beginning his march due to an ammunition wagon breaking down. He notified Floyd of the delay and requested additional wagons be sent to assist his movement. Floyd replied that he did not have sufficient wagons for his own command and none could therefore be spared. The turnpike had become exceedingly muddy from recent rains and progress was slow. Confederate infantry forces had advanced only nine miles to a position known as Locust Lane after an all day march. The cavalry, however, had advanced almost 26 miles and had clashed twice with the enemy.[23]

In the first fight Floyd's cavalry attacked and defeated a small band of Federals along the Sunday Road, a few miles away from General Cox and his entire army. Cox knew of the Confederate advance from scouting reports and he had posted cavalry and infantry detachments in various areas to sound the alarm when the Rebels approached. The Yankees lost two killed, five wounded and five captured on Sunday Road. Confederate losses were comparatively light with only a few wounded.[24]

As the main body of Floyd's cavalry advanced along the turnpike within a few miles of Gauley Bridge, they rode carelessly into an ambush set up by Colonel Frizell of the 11th Ohio Infantry. This was the same officer whose men had ambushed the Rebels at Sewell Mountain on the 15th. As the Rebel cavalry commanded by Col. St. George Croghan drew near, the Yankees opened fire. Taken by surprise, the Confederates returned fire but were thrown into confusion. Just as the Yankees had been outnumbered in the fight on Sunday Road, the Rebels here were outnumbered five to one. Colonel Croghan attempted to restore order amid the smoke and sound of battle but mass confusion prevailed as he watched four of his men emptied from their saddles. Two of his horses took off in a wild gallop away from the scene of action, splashing up the muddy road and carrying with them weapons and supplies the poor Confederates could not afford to lose. Somehow in all the confusion and flying lead Croghan's men managed to capture two Yankee's and kill two others. The Confederates made good their escape and reported the event to General Floyd whom they found several miles to the east along the turnpike.[25]

When General Cox was informed of the fighting and learned its proximity to his own position, he became increasingly concerned that a superior force of the enemy might attempt to drive him from his positions in the valley and adjacent country. After the Sewell Mountain skirmish of the 15th, he had written to Gen. William S. Rosecrans, who was then headquartered at Clarksburg, WV, and requested large quantities of ammunition and artillery supplies. The nearby fighting of the 20th further convinced Cox that his position was in peril and he began consolidating his forces. He fully understood that it was simply a matter of time before his army and the enemy would clash in more than a brief skirmish. It was about this time that Cox became overly cautious and in calling in some of his forces from the surrounding country, he actually opened a door for General Floyd to walk through.[26]

The 7th Ohio Infantry, commanded by Col. Erastus B. Tyler had been posted about a days march from Gauley Bridge, at Kesslers Cross Lanes, near Carnifex Ferry, Nicholas County. When Cox ordered them to Twenty Mile Creek, nearer his own position, General Floyd realized an important link in the Union army's chain of communications had been left unguarded. During the evening of Aug. 21 Floyd's army advanced down Sunday Road, past the scene of their skirmish, and crossed the Gauley River via Carnifex Ferry. In this way he had interposed his army between Cox and the Federal forces in Northwest Virginia under Rosecrans. General Wise encamped a few miles from Floyd at the intersection of the turnpike and the Sunday Road, a position known as Dogwood Gap or present-day Hico.[27]

From General Lee's camp at Valley Mountain he issued Special Orders number 243 on Aug. 21. This order was made necessary by the petty bickering of his subordinates, Wise and Floyd. In it, Lee designated the specific command structure for all Confederate forces then operating in Fayette and adjacent counties of West Virginia. The order placed command of all troops other than the Wise Legion, including the 2,100-man militia forces of Beckley and Chapman, to General Floyd.[28]

Floyd's new position was upon the north bluffs of the Gauley River, about a days march from, and in the rear of, General Cox. Floyd designated this Camp Gauley and the next day wrote to Lee informing him of his activities and asking for three regiments to replace the Wise Legion. The animosity and lack of cooperation between Floyd and Wise were greatly hampering Confederate efforts in the region and both men acknowledged it.[29]

General Cox did not learn the location of Floyd's army until Aug. 24, two full days after the Rebels had taken the position. Had it not been for the industrious efforts of Colonel Tyler's scouts, he may not have known their location for several more days. General Cox wrote immediately to Colonel Frizell informing him of the discovery and preparing for defense: "A note from Colonel Tyler informs me that a force of the enemy has got across the Gauley

8

River, near Cross Lanes. Inform Major Hines of this at once, and counsel with him whether our operation by the Sunday Road is a favorable one to aid Tyler. Let me hear from you early in the morning. Four or five companies under Major Hines and Coleman might go down that road and by cleaning out what they find, help Tyler considerably."[30]

It would prove too late for Cox's troops to "clean out" the Rebels. They did garner one small victory the following day, Sunday, Aug. 25, when a 175-man detachment of Floyd's cavalry commanded by Col. Albert Gallatin Jenkins, rode into another ambush set up by Colonel Frizell. Jenkins and his men had carelessly advanced along the Sunday Road beyond the area secured by the Wise Legion, and went boldly along the turnpike in the direction of Gauley Bridge. Colonel Frizell knew of their approach and he secreted his men in the woods along the road near a position known as the Hawks Nest. Once again the unsuspecting Confederates rode directly among the Yankees and when their column was about half surrounded, the Yanks opened fire.

Instantly, several Confederates fell from their horses and Colonel Jenkins' horse was shot under him. A complete state of panic came over the Rebels and many of them threw down their guns, knapsacks, canteens, and anything that would impede their flight. Some of the men managed to return fire but they were so completely surprised and surrounded they had no chance of success. When the smoke cleared, Jenkins' cavalry had suffered a humiliating defeat. Sixteen Confederates were wounded and one killed. Two of the wounded were so badly shot up they could not escape and were taken prisoner. Colonel Jenkins was also wounded, having been severely bruised in the fall from his horse. The Rebels also lost three horses, 20 hats, two saddles, and miscellaneous equipment that had been left strewn along the road. Federal losses were comparatively light with only a few wounded and none killed.[31]

General Floyd's Confederates had been thoroughly embarrassed, but his revenge was swift and sure. The following day, Aug. 26, a large body of Rebels attacked and thoroughly defeated Col. Erastus Tyler's 7th Ohio Infantry at Cross Lanes. Tyler had failed to post sufficient pickets or properly scout the area, even though he had been advised that Floyd's entire army was but three miles away. The victorious Confederates reported at least two Yankees killed, 29 wounded and 110 captured. More importantly, they had completely routed the 7th Ohio from their encampment and pursued them into the mountains.[32]

When news of Tyler's defeat reached Gen. George B. McClellan, he was furious. He ordered General Rosecrans to proceed south from Clarksburg and attack Floyd. This movement by Rosecrans into Nicholas County set the stage for the battle of Carnifex Ferry, and subsequently brought about the Sewell Mountain Campaign.

With Blue and Gray troops camped within such close proximity of each other, skirmishes continued in the area for the next week, culminating in an all day fight on Tuesday, Sept. 3rd. In this series of battles, General Wise with 1,250 men attacked the Yankees at Big Creek, west of Hawks Nest, while Gen. Augustus Chapman's 19th Brigade Virginia Militia, 1,500 strong, attacked the enemy near the Kanawha River below their headquarters at Gauley Bridge.

This two-pronged attack, east and west of General Cox's headquarters, caused him a great deal of discomfort and no little worry. Cox grew concerned that General Floyd would join in the attack by marching south along the Gauley River to come in above him. This proved not to be the case however, and the fighting ceased at dusk. The Federals suffered a total of six men wounded and three captured in the combined attacks. Confederate loses were 11 men killed and wounded.[33]

That evening as both sides regrouped, they held virtually the same positions they had held when the attacks began. The Confederates did garner some valuable information as to the strength and locations of the enemy, but not much else was accomplished.

General Lee had hoped the combined forces of Wise, Chapman and Beckley, would be able to push down the south side of the Kanawha River and procure salt from the Kanawha Salines near Malden.[34] It would seem on initial examination that the Rebel forces were strong enough at this time to meet Lee's expectations. The factors which must be considered in their failure are several in number, but mainly, the poor condition of the troops due to lack of sufficient supplies and medical stores, and the fact that so early in the war troops on both sides were "green" and time was needed before they would display the military talents which later crowned their efforts.

10

FIELD AND STAFF OFFICERS OF WISES LEGION
AUGUST 1861
Brig Genl/ Henry A. Wise
Asst Adjt Genl/ Capt. Wm. B. Tabb
Aid de Camp/ W. Bacon
Asst QM of Brigade/ Capt. F. D. Cleary
Asst Commissary/ Capt. Wm. H. Thomas

CORP OF ENGINEERS
Chief/ Capt. Bolton
        Capt. T. T. L. Snead
        1st. Lt. George Bagwell
        1st. Lt. Arch Blair
        2nd. Lt. S. A. M. Syme
Chief of Ordnance for Brigade/ Capt. L. Buckholtz
Medical Director/ Surgeon A. O. Crenshaw

CAVALRY REGIMENT
Colonel/ J. Lucius Davis
Lt. Col./ John N. Clarkson
Major/ C. B. Duffield
Adjutant/ M. J. Dimmock
Asst. QM./ S. C. Ludington
Asst. Commissary/ J. H. Vandiver

CORPS OF ARTILLERY
Lt. Col./ W. H. Gibbs
Adjutant/ C. Ellis Munford
Asst. QM./ L. N. Webb
Asst. Commissary/ John Mason

1st. REGIMENT INFANTRY
Colonel/ John H. Richardson
Lt. Col./ Nat Tyler
Major/ H. W. Fry
Adjutant/ Lt. Henry A. Wise
Asst. QM./ N. S. Thomas
Asst. Commissary/ A. Kinney

2nd. REGIMENT INFANTRY
Colonel/ C. F. Henningsen
Lt. Col./ F. P. Anderson
Major/ John Lawson
Adjutant/ Lt. John R. Blocker
Asst. QM./ J. C. Deane
Asst. Commissary/ A. W. Matthews

3rd. REGIMENT INFANTRY
Lt. Col./ James W. Spalding
Acting Major/ Capt. W. A. Swank
Adjutant/ Lt. J. H. Pearce
Asst. QM./ Joseph M. Brown
Asst. Commissary/ Huston Estill

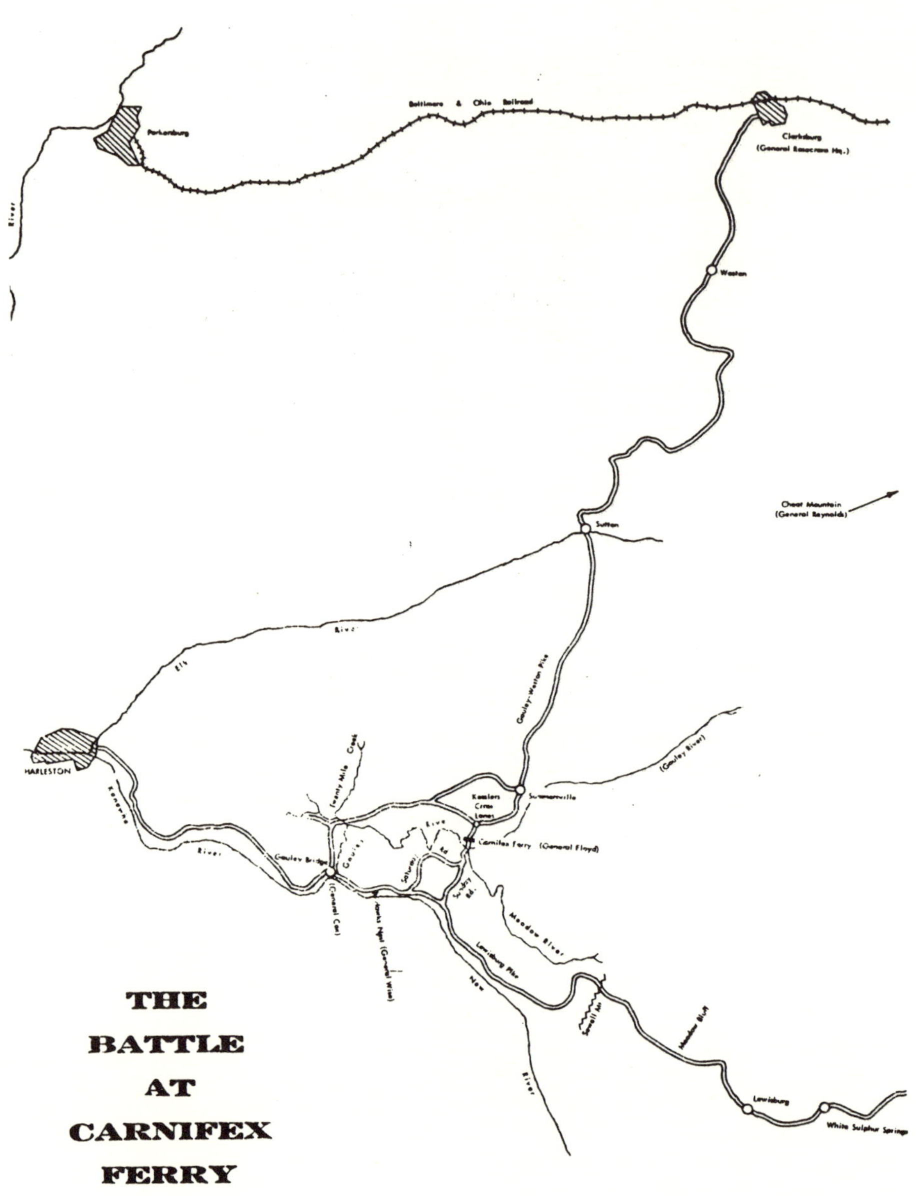

THE
BATTLE
AT
CARNIFEX
FERRY

Col. Joseph W. Frizell of the 11th Ohio Infantry. His men ambushed
Confederate cavalry at Sewell Mountain and Hawks Nest. FROM
HORTON & TEVERBAUGHS, HISTORY OF THE 11TH OVI - 1866

Zachariah Johnson of the 3rd Rgt. Wise Legion. He enlisted at Gauley Bridge, June 1861. COURTESY ROBERT BECKEL-HEIMER, OAK HILL, WV

Camp Gauley Bridge, 1861. COURTESY FAYETTE COUNTY HISTORICAL SOCIETY

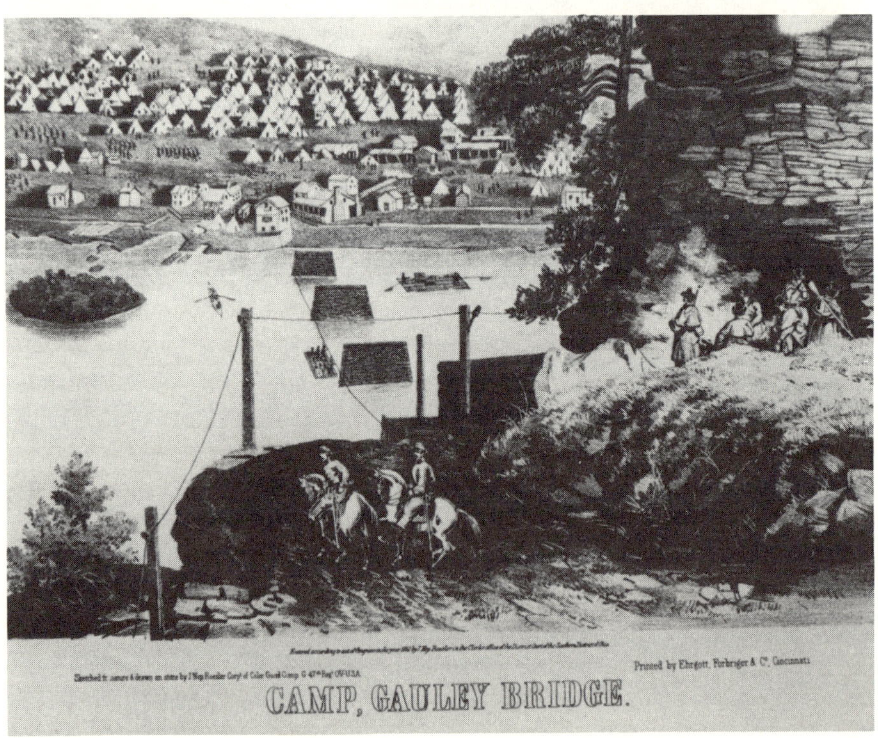

Previously unpublished view of Federal pickets near Gauley Bridge.
COURTESY SWV

Previously unpublished view of the wire suspension bridge which spanned the river at Gauley Bridge in 1862. This bridge had been built by the Federal Government to replace the one destroyed by Confederates prior to the Sewell Mountain campaign. COURTESY SWV

Carnifex Ferry to Sewell Mountain

After the skirmishes of Sept. 3, both sides busied themselves in scouting and entrenching their positions. On Sunday, Sept. 8, General Cox sent a dispatch to General Rosecrans, who was then on the march towards Summersville to assist Cox: "Wise is now encamped about two miles above Hawks Nest: has three pieces of cannon...his force not more than 2,500 I think...three regimental colors are flying in their camp."[1]

General Rosecrans was advancing with the expressed purpose of driving General Floyd from his entrenched position on the Gauley River and reopening the Federal line of communications between the Kanawha Valley and northwest Virginia. Rosecrans had with him an army of 5,000 men and boys. They arrived within striking distance of General Floyd on Sept. 9 but were yet unsure as to Floyd's exact location. Rosecrans had been told by various people along his route of march that Floyd was either at Carnifex Ferry or Cross Lanes. Being in a hostile country the Federals had to remain skeptical of any information passed onto them by the local citizens.

General Floyd had received reliable information concerning the advance of Rosecrans and he requested reinforcements from Wise. Floyd also had been promised by the Confederate authorities at Richmond that at least two regiments, the 13th Georgia and 14th North Carolina Infantries, would be with him shortly. As it turned out, only the 22nd Virginia Infantry, sent by General Wise, arrived in time for the battle of Carnifex Ferry. Even with the addition of the 22nd Virginia, Floyd's total army was only about 1,900. With this ill-equipped, poorly trained, and undisciplined force, Floyd faced almost certain destruction at the hands of General Rosecrans eager troops, who outnumbered him almost three to one.

The Confederate defensive line at Camp Gauley was designed in the shape of a horseshoe, with an earthen redoubt located at the front of the camp. The redoubt was approximately 312 feet long and included a parapet battery, 350 feet in front and center, from which the Rebel artillery had been positioned so as to fire over the parapet. A trench protected the battery epaulement. On both sides of the redoubt had been constructed high fences of wooden stakes, known as palisades. Log breastworks, used to screen the exterior slopes of the camp, were in a direct line with the front and curves of the defensive line. The left flank, which included more open ground than the right, was some 4,359 feet in length and had a double line of breastworks for added protection. The right flank was about equal in length to the left, and was more easily defended due to the slope directly in advance of it. Both flanks, as well as the majority of the battlefield, were covered with dense forest growth, a heavy undergrowth of laurel thickets, ravines, and rocky terrain. The road to the ferry led directly up the earthen redoubt over a natural glacis.

General Floyd was confident that in this strongly entrenched position he could defeat any force thrown against him. As one might expect, General Wise was not in the least impressed with Floyd's position. Wise said the "entrenchments were most unskillfully traced behind works not worthy of Chinese" and that Floyd's "breastworks were near woods all around except in front, and the enemy could approach him quite near." He closed his remarks by saying "Floyd cannot fight a superior force in any entrenchments that he has selected or constructed."[2]

Early in the afternoon of Sept. 10, Gen. Henry Benham, acting on orders of General Rosecrans, advanced nearer the positions believed held by Floyd's army. Benham's force consisted of the 10th Regiment Ohio Infantry. After moving only a short distance Benham reported discovering the enemy "through the opening of the woods on our left, their entrenchments in an open space beyond a deep and steep valley and crowning the crest of the opposite hill."[3] Sometime between 3 and 3:15 p.m., the entire Confederate line, artillery included, opened up on Benham and the 10th Ohio in a surprisingly ferocious barrage of iron and lead.

Lt. James T. Hickey of the 10th Ohio described the opening volleys of the battle: "They opened fire with rifle and musketry, grape and canister, shot and shell. There was not an inch of ground, a tree, nor a blade of grass that did not receive its share of fire."

General Benham quickly sent word to Rosecrans that reinforcements were desperately needed. Rosecrans responded immediately but Benham's men had been so far in the advance that it required almost an hour for reinforcements to arrive. Col. William Lytle of the 10th Ohio felt the full weight of combat as he watched his men fall around him: "their entire battery opened on us with grape and canister with almost paralyzing effect, my men falling around me in great numbers."[4]

Before Rosecrans and the others could reach the scene of action, Colonel Lytle determined to make a general assault upon the Confederate line. Sitting astride his black charger and waving his sword, Lytle turned sideways to his men and ordered: "Forward, follow. Men of the Tenth. Advance the colors." The men did advance, halting within pistol range of the Rebel artillerymen. Just at that instant Lytle received a bullet wound in the calf of his left leg. The bullet passed through his leg and killed his horse. Despite his injury and fall to the ground, Lytle continued giving orders to his men while under a murderous enemy fire. He gave orders until growing faint from the loss of blood. Lytle's gallantry even impressed the Rebels, as one of them later recorded: "I saw the daring officer fall from his horse and he was certainly one of the bravest of the brave, for he sought the bubble reputation at the very cannons mouth."[5]

As Yankee reinforcements began to arrive and their artillery commenced returning fire, the entire scene heated up considerably, as described by Capt. Robert Snead of Company F, 50th Virginia Infantry: "...at this time our cannon sent a fearful shot amongst them and did great destruction...boom went the cannon of our enemy, the large balls whistling over our heads, our men flat on the ground, then a volley of musketry would follow and then a round of cannon; then came a terrible shot of shell, it burst and fell all around us...about thirty feet to my right a large chestnut was struck and cut nearly in two...then another, I think a 12 pounder, tore the top of an oak tree to pieces. Just ahead of us, the bullets fell like rain whistling and whizzing over our heads and into the logs we lay behind."[6]

As the battle raged on tactical mistakes and blunders committed by the Yankees resulted in the gruesome death of Col. John W. Lowe, of the 12th Ohio Infantry. Lowe's death came as his men appeared almost directly in front of the Rebel artillery. Lowe ordered his men to advance to the right and just as he raised his sword above his head and ordered: "Follow me, my men. Charge." an enemy bullet entered the center of his forehead, right between his eyes, killing him instantly. As Lowe's body lay on the ground his legs were shattered with canister, and his entire body was later found to be mutilated from enemy fire.

There was no shortage of heroics on either side in this fight and the Confederates of General Floyd proudly boasted of their accomplishments. Such as the incident involving Peter Otey of the 51st Virginia Infantry. Otey saw a wounded comrade galloping forward on horseback while under severe fire by the enemy. Ignoring danger, Otey went out and retrieved the man.[7]

During the course of the afternoon and early evening the Federal troops made several bold assaults upon the Rebel line. Each assault met the same result, failure. General Floyd's earthworks and plans had apparently been every bit as strong as he had believed. Finally, near 7 p.m. with darkness at hand, General Rosecrans ordered the final assault. This decision to continue the fight cost Rosecrans dearly.

While attempting to maneuver in the mountain darkness in uneven and unfamiliar terrain, detachments of the 13th, 23rd, and 28th Ohio Infantries, had somehow formed themselves into a "U" shape. As they stumbled along in an attempt to reach their point of attack a lone shot rang out in the night. Suddenly everyone began firing and in a few minutes it was discovered that the 13th and 23rd Ohio regiments had fired into the 28th Ohio. When calm was restored it was found that the Yankees had killed two and wounded 30 of their own men. Needless to say, this tragedy put an end to the planned night attack. General Rosecrans ordered his army to establish defensive perimeters and encamp. He then set about planning the next day's assault.

That evening Floyd called a council of war with his officers. He knew that in all the enemy assaults and probing they had discovered the weaknesses in his line, and he was sure his men could not resist another days round of enemy attacks. Therefore, Floyd decided to retreat during the night by using Carnifex Ferry and a foot bridge there to cross the Gauley into Fayette County. Had the enemy discovered his retreat, Floyd's entire command may have been annihilated. Miraculously, the Yankees did not discover the movement, and dawn of Sept. 11 found Floyd's Confederates several miles away, having destroyed the ferry and foot bridge as they left.

At 6 a.m. Federal troops under Gen. Hugh B. Ewing advanced to the Rebel position and discovered it abandoned. Still flying defiantly over the breastworks was a Confederate flag which was taken. On the flag was the gold-lettered inscription: FLOYD'S BRIGADE/THE PRICE OF LIBERTY IS THE BLOOD OF THE BRAVE. The Yankees also found at the site large quantities of supplies, including muskets. Twenty-five members of Col. Tyler's 7th Ohio Infantry, captured on Aug. 26 at Cross Lanes, were retaken, along with several sick and wounded Confederates.

Rosecrans men had suffered 27 killed, 103 wounded and four missing in the battle. Surprisingly, no Confederates were killed, only seven wounded and 17 captured.[8] Both Floyd and Rosecrans claimed victory at Carnifex Ferry, and both had good arguments to support their claims. One important factor remained in favor of the Federals. By forcing the Rebels to abandon Camp Gauley, the Union army's line of communication between Sutton and Gauley Bridge was reopened. Also, a severe blow had been dealt the Confederate ideal in western Virginia by making it possible for the loyal government of Virginia to meet in Wheeling in October. that meeting paved the way for West Virginia statehood.

General Floyd's army withdrew along the Sunday Road and met General Wise near present day Hico. Floyd was understandably upset that Wise had failed to reinforce him in time for the battle. Actually, Wise did send one regiment and retained the balance of his command to prevent the enemy from attacking Floyd's rear via the Sunday Road and Carnifex Ferry. Wise's troops were attacked in their position on the Sunday Road as the larger battle was underway. Had they not been where they were, it is conceivable that Floyd's men would have been caught in a pincer movement and very possibly destroyed. Floyd's agitation prompted him to write a letter on Sept. 12 to L.P. Walker, the Confederate Secretary of War.[9] Coincidentally, the Southern authorities at Richmond sent a dispatch to General Lee on that same date, authorizing Lee to replace Wise: "I am instructed by the President to say that you have authority to transfer General Wise's Legion proper to any other command than that of General Floyd...it being clearly evident that the commands of Generals Floyd and Wise cannot cooperate with any advantage to the service. The absence of General Wise's Legion from the future operations of General Floyd will be replaced by orders from here for Colonel Russell's Twentieth Mississippi Volunteers and Colonel Phillip's Georgia Legion, both at Lynchburg, to join Floyd."[10]

The two Rebel armies continued their retreat until reaching

Walkers, a private residence and occasional stagecoach stop along the turnpike near the western top of Sewell Mountain. At this point Floyd determined to hold a council of war, and sent Wise a dispatch asking him to attend: "It becomes necessary that a prompt and definite line of action should be at once determined upon and executed. May I ask the favor of you to come down this evening, and bring such officers as you choose to join us in council. Thus we may determine what is best to be done and put the plan into execution at once."[11]

As a result of this war council, Floyd issued orders for the entire command to fall back several more miles to the top of Big Sewell Mountain, which was accomplished the next day. General Floyd also issued orders at this time directing that the Allegheny College, at Blue Sulphur Springs in Greenbrier County, be established as a hospital for the sick and wounded of the Army of the Kanawha.[12] (It should be noted that orders of this period were signed by Floyd's adjutant, as Floyd was slightly wounded in the right arm at Carnifex.) This movement away from the Kanawha Valley was not done entirely without the Yankees knowledge. Rosecrans and Cox had sent numerous scouts and spies out into the countryside after the battle of Carnifex Ferry, with orders to report the activities of the Rebels. They had also dispatched two regiments to the area recently occupied by the Wise Legion in the mistaken hope that they could prevent a union of the two Southern commands.

Floyd had learned on the 11th that the two regiments sent by Richmond to reinforce him, the 13th Georgia and 14th North Carolina Infantry, were then encamped four miles west of the Sewell Mountain range. He ordered them to establish camp at Frank Tyree's and await further orders. As his army marched to Big Sewell, the reinforcements were met and joined the main body of troops. This swelled Floyd's effective force by several hundred men. It also increased his need for supplies, an increasingly severe problem in a region already drained of food for the men and forage for the animals. In fact, Blue and Gray troops alike were finding it difficult to survive in this rugged wilderness, and matters would only grow worse in the coming weeks. Western Virginia was a land of breathtaking beauty, but a land cruel to armies. The region about Sewell Mountain proved especially so with its jumbled terrain of heavily timbered ridges, covered in thick laurel, rhododendron, and ground pine.

As the Confederate forces regrouped at Big Sewell on Sept. 14, the Southern militiamen of Generals Beckley and Chapman withdrew from their camps at Fayetteville, with Beckley's men returning to their base of operations at Raleigh Courthouse (Beckley). Once established in camp at Sewell General Floyd ordered detachments of cavalry out into the countryside. His cavalry was so diminished by disease and the lack of provender for the animals, that he was forced to ask Wise for assistance: "It is essential that the turnpike west of this point should be watched and scouted tonight, in order that I may reliably and speedily be informed of the advance of the enemy. My cavalry are all on the Wilderness Road, under Colonel Croghan...of the companies of Captains Corn and Beckett only 10 fit for service. These 10 have been already sent upon the turnpike west...this force is entirely inadequate for a proper scout. You will therefore detail from your cavalry 20 men, to proceed upon the turnpike."[13]

Rather than 20 men, Wise ordered only 12 cavalrymen out along the turnpike to watch for the enemy's advance. These men returned to camp too soon to ensure the safety of their combined commands, and this resulted in another round of complaints between Wise and Floyd on the 15th.[14] Later that same day, as Floyd busied himself with the minutiae of military administration, he wrote again to President Davis, complaining about Wise: "Things have assumed a complexion here which require your prompt and immediate action. The petty jealousy of General Wise; his utter ignorance of all military rule and discipline; the peculiar contrariness of his character and disposition, are beginning to produce rapidly a disorganization which will prove fatal to the interest of the army if not arrested at once...It is impossible for me to conduct a campaign with General Wise attached to my command."[15]

Burdens continued to mount for General Floyd when he received a letter from Gen. Augustus A. Chapman, of the 19th Brigade Virginia Militia, stating that morale was very poor among his troops: "...they are much disheartened by the retreat and I fear I shall hardly be able to keep them embodied when they get in the neighborhood of home."[16] Also on the 15th, the following from General Beckley concerning his militia: "I have reached this place (Raleigh Courthouse) pursuant to your orders, but I am sorry to say with a very diminished force. The Fayette Regiment has been reduced by desertion from some 280 men to between 50 and 100 men. My men are much fatigued and we are without tents or cartridge boxes; dependent upon vacant homes for shelter. With great respect I would ask that the orders requiring me to join your forces and General Wise's, be suspended until I can rest and recruit my small brigade."[17]

Desertion was a problem throughout the war for Blue and Gray alike, but it was more so very early in the conflict. The Southern men had joined the army intent upon protecting their own families and property. When the tide of war swept them from their own domain, they frequently did not feel obliged to go. This was not from a lack of patriotism or devotion to the ideals espoused by the Southern Confederacy. It was to them more a matter of common sense and devotion to family. As the war dragged on and the novelty of the experience faded, this became less and less a problem, although desertions of course, remained a fact of military life.

Other facts of military life contributed to General Floyd's agitation. Such seemingly trivial details as the amount of baggage carried by the troops, required the time and action of the commanding general: "The general commanding notices that in many instances the amount of baggage belonging to officers and others of this command is altogether too large. Trunks are forbidden to be transported with the army. Colonels of regiments will cause all the trunks and surplus articles of baggage to be sent to Lewisburg. The amount of bedding and clothing and cooking utensils allowed to be carried will not exceed 30 pounds."[18] In closely examining available records, we can see that General Floyd had not yet mastered the art of delegating authority. He allowed himself to become so entangled in military minutiae that it even fell to him to order out the pickets: "The Colonels of the 22nd, 36th, 45th, 50th, 51st Virginia Regiments and of the 13th Georgia and 14th North Carolina Regiments will each have detailed three privates from his regiment as relief to the picket on duty last night. The detail will report to Colonel Reid at the gaps leading into the encampments on each side of the pike. Officers of the 14th North Carolina Infantry will furnish one lieutenant, one sergeant; The 13th Ga--two corporals."[19]

General Rosecrans was not immune to many of the same problems which plagued Floyd. Rosecrans found the western Virginia countryside so difficult to travel with a large force that he soon realized he could not supply his army by wagon train. The route from Clarksburg to the Kanawha Valley was a long and difficult journey.

So much so that it was decided the Kanawha River must be made the line of supply and communication with his base, which he transferred to Gallipolis, Ohio. It remained at that location throughout the Sewell Mountain campaign.

General Cox had anticipated Rosecrans' decision and had accumulated large quantities of supplies and ordnance stores at Gauley Bridge. In an effort to facilitate the smooth operation of his supply points, and realizing a need to discuss his plans with his subordinates, Rosecrans held a council of war at Cross Lanes about noon of the 15th. Gen. Jacob D. Cox later described the meeting: "I rode over from my camp at the Sunday Road...and passing through the field of the recent combat, reached the general's headquarters...I was able to assure him that it was easy for his command to follow the line of march on which Floyd had retreated, if better means of crossing the Gauley were provided....He hesitated to commit himself...McCook's brigade was ordered to report to me as soon as it could be put over the river, and I was authorized to advance some six miles (from Sunday Road) toward the enemy, to Aldersons or Spy Rock...beyond which Sewell Mountain is 14 miles southeast."[20]

The scene of action switched to the Sewell Mountain range with the advance of General Cox. His formidable army of approximately 5,000 men reached Spy Rock just before dark of Sept. 16. The Federal infantry, cavalry, and artillery, occupied a large field just beyond the home of George Alderson, on the right of the turnpike. Alderson's house was used as Cox's headquarters.[21]

George Alderson was 70 years old, a former colonel of Virginia militia, and a strong Confederate sympathizer. He operated a toll gate and stagecoach stop at Spy Rock or present day Lookout. He had been actively and peacefully engaged in that enterprise since 1834. Obviously, having a host of Yankees occupy his house and property was not to his liking. Making matters worse was the fact that Alderson's son was active in the Confederate Government at Richmond. All these facts were of course well known to the Yankees and undoubtedly contributed greatly to the rough treatment the old colonel received at the mercy of his unwelcome guests. From papers now in possession of Colonel Alderson's descendants, we can learn something of the price many civilians paid as they were visited by this "unnatural war:"

Memo of Loss at DeKalb Fayette Va by the enemy, Sept 1861 viz

140 head of sheep @ $3	$420
4 milk cows @ $20	$ 80
1 Durham Bull	$ 50
9 calves @ $8	$ 72
6 Yearlings @ $20	$120
2 (illegible) @ $100	$200
5 fat hogs in pen	$ 60
2 Sows and 9 Shoats	$ 20
13 Geese	$ 6.50
31 Ducks	$ 6.25
22 Turkeys @ .75	$ 16.50
50 Hens & Roosters	$ 16.34
Grain & Hay	
	$1,034.59

As if these losses were not bad enough, the lists go on to include such items as seven acres of buckwheat, 20 acres of corn, 100 bushels of potatoes, and other food, valued at almost $600. Adding insult to injury, the "damned yankees" even took most of the Alderson's furniture, books, household supplies such as candles and oil, and even farming and blacksmithing tools. The total value of all items stolen by the enemy during September 1861 is given as $4,664.09. Needless to say these losses put the Aldersons temporarily out of the innkeeping business, and almost out of the survival business.[22]

The Alderson family documents also show that when Floyd's cavalry encamped at Spy Rock during August, they paid the old colonel for everything they used. Their first night at DeKalb (the name of the inn) was Aug. 19 as their army advanced toward the Kanawha Valley. The lists show that Mr. Alderson was paid $107.91 for two nights and two days of hay; 218 pounds of beef; one bushel of potatoes; 26 "diets to privates" priced at .25 cents each; five acres of oats; two additional acres of oats and hay. This cavalry was commanded by Col. St. George Croghan (who was killed in November 1861 by the enemy).

26

On the morning of Sept. 16 General Floyd received reliable information that the Yankees were advancing toward his position, and may attempt to flank his command via the Wilderness Road, which terminated at Meadow Bluff. Realizing the urgency of the situation, Floyd ordered Col. G.F. Henry to obstruct the road: "I think it proper to say to you that it becomes a matter of vital importance to prevent, if possible, and if not possible to prevent, then certainly to retard, the advance of the enemy upon the Wilderness Road....one of the best modes by which it can be done is for you to go down as far as possible on the Wilderness Road with all your force and spare no pains or labor to obstruct it completely. The closer these obstructions are to the river, the more desirable it is, and every point should be obstructed where such a thing is possible."[23]

Floyd then ordered 50 privates, one captain, and two lieutenants, be sent from each regiment under his command to assist Col. Gabriel C. Wharton, who was in charge of "the works of fortification now in progress."[24] Early that afternoon General Floyd determined that a council of war was necessary. He sent a notice to General Wise asking his presence at the meeting "at as early an hour this afternoon as possible." At 5 p.m. Wise and four of his officers, including his son, Capt. Obadiah J. Wise (who was killed in February 1862) arrived at Floyd's headquarters tent for the meeting. As usual this was not a cordial affair, although it was an informative one, in that detailed discussions were held concerning all aspects of the campaign then underway. General Wise explained that he would like to make an advance down the left (south) bank of the Kanawha River, pushing his way to Charleston with a large force of cavalry and infantry from their combined commands. He also stated firmly that he believed the positions now held by their forces should be maintained at least a few more days, until the intentions of the enemy could be more accurately determined.

After conferring almost two hours the meeting adjourned with an apparent agreement between Floyd and Wise to maintain their present positions. At this point it appears that General Floyd either had a change of heart, or had intentionally deceived Wise as to his actual plans. Within a very short period after the meeting, perhaps less than one hour, General Floyd issued orders for his command to withdraw immediately. He also ordered Wise to fall back as his column passed: "I am instructed by General Floyd to say to you that it has been determined to fall back to the most defensible point between Meadow Bluff and Lewisburg. He will put his column in motion at once. You will hold your command in readiness to bring up the rear."[25]

This apparent deception on the part of Floyd infuriated Wise and he very defiantly refused to budge from his camp, which he named "Camp Defiance." All this of course resulted in another series of letters between these two political generals. In one of the letters Wise explained his astonishment to Floyd: "...this order to be ready followed immediately after a verbal conference with you, at your request, in which I understood you distinctly as determining to hold, for a time at least, the almost impregnable position which I now occupy...We had hardly ridden to my headquarters...when wagons came moving back...My camp has many sick, some convalescent, and I deem it inhumane to risk the health of these men in this wet weather."[26]

As Floyd's haggard army passed the camps of the Wise Legion on their surprise night march, Wise made it a point to curse Floyd in front of the legion, as recorded by Col. Henry Heth: "...Wise got on his horse and rode to his command, where he halted, raised himself in his stirrups, and in a stentorian voice called out 'Who is retreating now?' He rode slowly on, and seeing another group of his men, he repeated the same to them. Presently, his entire command had assembled and he said, 'Men, who is retreating now? John B. Floyd, damn him, the bullet hit son of a bitch, he is retreating now.'"[27]

The night of Sept. 16 was an especially dark and dismal one, and certainly not a good night to march more than a short distance. Recent rains had transformed the so-called turnpike into a virtual sea of mud and clouds kept the moon and stars from view. The wagon train, over one mile in length, and the artillery pieces, were difficult to manage even in daylight on a good road. Under these conditions the task was tedious beyond description and many of Floyd's officers and men were angered by the move, which certainly could have waited until morning. Troops of the Wise Legion quietly watched as their disgruntled comrades marched off into the mountain darkness, their columns lit only by an occasional torch. Lt. D.B. Baldwin of the 51st Virginia Infantry, described the arduous march in a letter to his wife: "That night about 10 O.C. I had gone to bed and was reading when we were ordered to strike tents and march for Meadow Bluff. We got our regiment into line about 11 O.C....it commenced raining and continued for several hours and the mud was so deep that the horses could not get along faster. We got here

(Meadow Bluff) yesterday at 12 O.C. got up our tents, and got supper at dark."[28]

Using the times listed in Baldwin's letter, we can see that General Floyd's troops took 13 hours to march the 14 or so miles from Big Sewell to Meadow Bluff. The majority of Floyd's sick troops, who were numerous, were left behind and the responsibility for their care fell upon General Wise.

General Cox was active on the 17th attempting to supply and organize his forces at Spy Rock. It was no small matter to feed and clothe 5,000 men, and several hundred horses. Many hours of diligent study and preparation were required to maintain an efficient operation of the army. Especially in view of the fact that the Rebels were but a few miles east of the Federal encampments and the threat of an attack weighed heavily upon the minds of officers and men alike. Cox very skillfully posted his pickets and kept an active cavalry force out in the direction of Sewell Mountain, as he explained in a dispatch to General Rosecrans: "We have made no forward movement today, McCook being in expectation of his train. Most of mine has arrived. My advance guard is at the foot of Sewell Mountain, and I expect it to report a reconnaissance to the summit. A scouting party of the enemy was on Sewell last night. Have heard of none nearer."[29]

General Cox also sent his assistant quartermaster a list of needed items: "We need a considerable supply of socks, also two travelling forges with smiths, & supply of horse shoes & iron, also all the remainder of tents and camp equipage of the men here. Also a supply of hats & overcoats for at least 5,000 men."[30] Capt. W.D. Loomis was Cox's assistant quartermaster and he apparently found the burden of his responsibilities too much to bear. Instead of forwarding the requested supplies, Loomis very brazenly wrote to Cox saying that the supply order was "more than I can bear" and "is not right." To this somewhat surprising response General Cox sent Loomis a six-page letter, in which he explained in detail the responsibilities of a quartermaster. He also made it clear to his subordinate that "You are under military orders from these headquarters, & the response to orders received by you must be as prompt, complete, & uncomplaining, as any officer of the line." Cox also threatened Loomis in saying: "...but a repetition of a petulant reply...will be followed by the immediate substitution of some other officer...while the matter is being submitted to a Court Martial."[31]

General Cox also wrote to Colonel Tyler, who was then at Gauley Bridge, ordering the establishment of a line of military couriers between Charleston and his headquarters at Spy Rock. These couriers were set up with relays of horses every 10 miles. The first relay east of Gauley Bridge was at the home of Matilda Hamilton, near the Hawks Nest Lodge in present day Hawks Nest State Park. The second relay was at Aldersons, with plans to continue at 10-mile intervals to the foot of Sewell Mountain. He also sent a dispatch to his commissary department which was then commanded by Capt. John B. Gibb: "...I shall rely upon you to keep supplied my own and Colonel McCook's command, say 5,000. Send us some salt, vinegar, molasses....I shall look for General Rosecrans to be on this line within two days...as soon as Genl R. comes I shall order you up."[32]

The camps of Floyd and Wise were also busy on the 17th, being engaged in resupply, organization, and entrenching work. General Wise received a letter from Dr. D.B. Phillips, his military surgeon, who was in charge of the Confederate hospital at White Sulphur Springs. Dr. Phillips asked permission to leave his post at various times without first notifying Wise. He also forwarded a general report as to the situation at the hospital, and seized the opportunity to complain about the rather ambiguous nature of his authority at that post. Wise knew that the efficient operation of his hospital posts was crucial to the overall success of the campaign. Even though the Confederate military had been operating in the mountains only a few weeks, the various military hospitals in the region were overcrowded and understaffed. Various ailments such as dysentery and typhoid would reach near epidemic proportions before the Sewell Mountain campaign was concluded. The almost constant rains and frequent winds combined with a general lack of shelter, spawned disease which took a toll on the Southern forces much greater than any Yankee bullets.

With the commands of Wise and Floyd separated, both commanders began focusing their attention on preparing their camps against attack. General Wise ordered all provisions and nonessential baggage wagons withdrawn to safe positions and the camp on all sides strengthened. On Sept. 18 Wise addressed the troops of his legion with a long patriotic speech intended to boost morale. He told his men that he had never retreated except in obedience to orders from his superiors, and that he was determined to make a stand at Sewell Mountain. Wise proclaimed that his troops must be prepared to fight an enemy superior in numbers by "two or three or several to one," and that they would probably be attacked front and rear for successive days. He concluded his remarks by offering to allow any man or officer under his command who would be doubtful as to the outcome of such a fight, to march at once to Meadow Bluff. Wise's speech had the desired effect, as described by a witness: "The speech, delivered successively to the three regiments of infantry and to the artillery, was received with the wildest enthusiasm. Not one solitary individual in the legion failed to respond, and the spirits of the corps were raised and maintained at the highest fighting pitch."[33]

Although Camp Defiance was rapidly being prepared for defense and talk of "making a stand" filled the mountain air, records show that General Wise was also busy on the 18th preparing to withdraw in a few days. He wrote to Capt. F.D. Cleary and W.H. Thomas of his quartermaster and commissary departments, instructing them to withhold supplies coming into his camp with the exception of corn and oats necessary for the horses. He also directed that all available wagons be sent to him to facilitate a move to "some point near Lewisburg." He ordered Captain Cleary to "bring on the empty wagons to this place, sufficient to supply ample transportation for each company & for all the QM & commissary stores & for ammunition...preferring ammunition and ordnance first, provisions and forage of grain next, baggage and clothing next and cooking utensils last. All the wagons necessary for the movement of everything will be ordered up."[34]

This apparent discrepancy between Wise's words and deeds may have been induced by the fact that General Floyd was still attempting to get Wise to join him at Meadow Bluff. In closely examining the available records it appears that Wise never gave his commander the satisfaction of saying that he would join him, although he obviously anticipated a movement nearer Lewisburg.

Being frustrated in his attempts to unite forces at Meadow Bluff, General Floyd ordered the militia of Gens. Chapman and Beckley to join him without delay. He explained to Chapman the latest activities of the enemy, saying that on "yesterday afternoon they threw a large force of infantry with cannon across the river at Carnifex Ferry. This force will unite certainly with that already on this side and attempt to fight a way to Lewisburg. In view, then, of my prospect of having to fight these two columns combined, you will put your command and that of General Beckley on the march, with a view to join me at the earliest practicable moment."[35]

As General Wise was busy ordering supplies halted pending a withdraw, General Cox was active in his camp on the 18th attempting to feed his troops. Cox found the situation at Spy Rock a rough one indeed and he told his commissary officer that "this country is perfectly stripped of food & forage & we must rely on the commissary and quartermaster for everything. Even at HQ we can procure nothing. There is nothing to be bought. We have found a few cattle & sheep which by the way the men need salt." The cattle and sheep which Cox says they "found" was undoubtedly that confiscated from the Alderson family. General Cox also stated that "we are in danger of being absolutely without food."[36]

On Thursday, Sept. 19, Cox ordered his scouting parties to probe into the wilderness as far as the foot of Sewell. This movement was an attempt to locate suitable camping grounds for the brigade, and the force sent out was quite large. Large enough in fact, that when Confederate scouts reported their presence in the area, Wise wrote Floyd saying that his scouts report "hearing their drums at the turnpike, at Sunday Road, and at Aldersons all this morning....I shall hold on here and fight the enemy, expecting them to attack me before sunrise this morning...and leave it to your better judgment to send reinforcements or not."[37]

To this notice from Wise General Floyd replied that he had known for several days about the enemy's advance and he again asked Wise to join him at Meadow Bluff, saying: "I regret exceedingly that you did not think proper to bring up my rear, as directed in my order of the 16th...disastrous consequences, which may ensue from a divided force, may result from this, ...if you still have time upon receipt of this, to join my force and make a stand against the enemy at this point, I hope you will see the necessity of doing so."[38]

Wise, of course, did not see things as his commander did, and replied that he had been ordered to be in readiness to move, but that no order to move was ever given. He followed that letter with another in which he described his ability to defeat the enemy: "I can meet them in the trenches with 1,800 infantry and artillery, and by tomorrow will have my eight companies of cavalry (say 350 to 400) in all, 2,200, with nine pieces of artillery. With this force, posted as I am, I can repulse 4,000."[39]

32

The petty bickering between these two political generals had caused considerable consternation among the civilians of southern West Virginia. President Davis had already received several letters of concern from various prominent citizens of Lewisburg. Mason Mathews, Greenbrier County representative to the Virginia Legislature, was among those who wrote Davis of their concerns: "I allude to the unfriendly relations existing between the two generals, Floyd and Wise...from their course and actions I am fully satisfied that each of them would be highly gratified to see the other annihilated....It would be just as easy to combine oil and water as to expect a union of action between these gentlemen."[40]

Being convinced that he would eventually fight the Yankees at Meadow Bluff, General Floyd ordered trenches dug along the eastern bank of Meadow River, about one mile west of his headquarters. These trenches were practically worthless for defense as the position was almost entirely surrounded by high hills from which an enemy could easily render the position untenable. Col. Augustus Forsberg of the 51st Virginia Infantry was placed in charge of the works and later described their construction: "My time was now occupied in superintending various small fortifications on the Meadow River and near camp, building new roads, and repairing old ones."[41] Another description of this work was written by William Clark Reynolds of the 22nd Virginia Infantry: "Our regiment worked on the breast works on the right flank of the Meadow River fortifications. Our company had one axe and two butcher knives to work with, so some idea may be formed of the efficiency of our defenses."[42]

Organization of the 19th Brigade Virginia Militia
August - September 1861

Brig. Gen. Augustus Alexandria Chapman - commanding six regiments
79th Regt. - Greenbrier Co. - Col. George F. Henry - five companies
86th Regt. - Giles Co. - LtC. James W. English - six companies
108th Regt. - Monroe Co. - Col. John M. Rowan - seven companies
135th Regt. - Greenbrier Co. - Col. John Snyder - six companies
151st Regt. - Mercer Co. - LtC. John S. Carr - six companies
166th Regt. - Monroe Co. - Col. William B. Suttle - nine companies

Organization of the 27th Brigade Virginia Militia
August - September 1861

Brig. Gen. Alfred Beckley - commanding six regiments
126th Regt - Nicholas Co. - two companies (estimated)
129th Regt - Nicholas & Logan Co. - Col. John Dejernatt - six companies
142nd Regt - Fayette Co. - Col. Samuel B. Woods - three companies
184th Regt - Raleigh Co. - three companies
187th Regt - Boone Co. - two companies
190th Regt - Wyoming Co. - Col. William N. Henderson - two companies

NOTE: As was usually the case with militia, these were very "light" companies. The two brigades while at Sewell Mountain contained 57 companies, totaling only about 2,100 men and officers, or an average of 36 men per company.

Col. George Alderson, proprietor of DeKalb, the inn and stagecoach stop at Lookout, WV. Union troops used the inn as headquarters during the Sewell Mountain campaign.

Gen. William S. Rosecrans, commander of the Union forces during
the Sewell Mountain campaign. AUTHOR'S COLLECTION

Previously unpublished view of "DeKalb," the inn operated by George Alderson at Lookout, WV Built in 1834, it was torn down in 1899. During the Sewell Mountain campaign the inn and property was occupied by Yankee troops. COURTESY TOM ALDERSON

Lee Takes Command

As the early morning sun of Sept. 20 broke through the mountain fog at Camp Lookout, General Cox sent a dispatch to Rosecrans. He advised his commander that everything was peaceful at his camp and at the position held by Major Hines, nearer Sewell Mountain. Cox also expressed concern about a secret trade in salt and beef cattle with the Rebels, that apparently was taking place in the counties between the Kanawha River and Wytheville. A few hours later, Cox again wrote Rosecrans to notify him that Major Hines had advanced to the western top of Sewell. Hines found there a line of entrenchments and fortifications which the Confederates had constructed during their retreat. He did not realize at that time that he had advanced to within one mile of the Wise Legion, and he told General Cox that it was believed that the Rebels were at Meadow Bluff, some 16 miles away. Cox told Rosecrans that he hoped to advance toward Sewell as soon as his transportation would permit. General Rosecrans replied later that same day, advising Cox to: "Let the advanced guard on Sewell examine and choose a strongly defensible position, and allow no passings whatever."[1]

At Camp Meadow Bluff, General Floyd received a letter from General Lee, saying that he was then at Frankford, east of Lewisburg: "I have reached this point on my way to your camp. Major Reynolds...informs me that it is believed the enemy in full force is crossing the Gauley River to attack you...Collect all your force and throw up such breast-works as you can to oppose him...send for General Chapman and Colonel Beckley to cross to your side...all your sick in rear of you ought to be sent well back. I have only a few cavalry with me and shall be obliged to halt for the night this side of Lewisburg."[2]

From various scouting reports General Wise knew that the enemy had advanced nearer his position. Believing that he might ascertain accurate information as to their strength, Wise determined to make an advanced scout, which he began in the later afternoon of Sept. 20. For this scout Wise selected five companies of infantry, totaling about 250 men. These included the Richmond Light Infantry Blues, of the 46th Virginia Infantry, commanded by Wise's son, Capt. O. Jennings Wise; and the bold Louisiana Rangers of Capt. William F. McClean, temporarily commanded by 20-year-old Capt. Francis M. Imboden, of the 59th Virginia Infantry.

After advancing but a short distance through the dense wilderness, Wise and his party came under a heavy skirmishing fire from advance elements of Cox's army. These were the men of Major Hines who had occupied their position only hours before, not knowing of their close proximity to the Confederates. Undaunted by such sudden enemy contact, General Wise and his men pressed forward through the thickets and tangled undergrowth. All around them the ravines reverberated with the sounds of musket and small arms fire. The Yankees fell back as Wise pressed the issue, driving in their pickets from behind rocks and trees. A lively skirmish was continued until nightfall required a halt, at which time Wise and his men made camp in a ravine. Here, in the mountain darkness, the Rebels realized they had occupied a "no mans land" between the opposing camps. In the skirmishing the Federals lost one man; the Confederates had no casualties.

That night occasional rain made it difficult to keep a fire and the temperatures were unseasonably cool. The intrepid Confederates slept under heavens canopy fully exposed to the elements, as they had failed to bring tents. At 5:30 the next morning Wise and company were awakened from their crude rest as the bugler's call for reveille pierced the damp mountain air and wound its way to their encampment.

General Wise promptly sent a dispatch back to Camp Defiance notifying his men there that he intended to press the enemy further. Already, he had gained valuable information as to the strength and locations of the Yankees, and Wise realized the time was right to reconnoiter his front as far as possible. Advancing on foot, contact was again made with the enemy, who had withdrawn only a short distance during the night. A running skirmish was kept up until the Yankees had been driven back about two miles from Camp Defiance, beyond a position known as the Kenny farm.

It had now reached early afternoon of the 21st and Wise ordered a return to camp, to which point they arrived about 5:00 p.m. Back at his headquarters Wise was given a dispatch from General Lee, who had just arrived at Meadow Bluff from Randolph County. Lee had been thoroughly briefed on the situation at both Southern camps by General Floyd, and he was not happy to find their forces still divided, as he explained to Wise: "I have just arrived at this camp and regret to find the forces not united...as far as I can judge our united forces are not more than one half of the strength of the enemy. Together they may not be able to withstand his assault. It would be the height of imprudence to submit them separately to his attack...I beg therefore, if not too late, that the troops be united, and that we conquer or die together. You have spoken to me of want of consultation and concert; let that pass until the enemy is driven back, and then, as far as I can, all shall be arranged. I expect this of your magnanimity. Consult that and the interest of our cause, and all will go well."[3]

Wise was offended by the tone and content of Lee's letter, and he responded accordingly: "I have just returned from feeling the enemy, being out all night and driving in their pickets this morning...but, wet, weary, and fatigued as I am, your note reads so much like a rebuke, which I do not think I deserve, that I do not...lose a moment without replying....In the first place, I consider my force united with that of General Floyd as much as it ever has been...Floyd has about 3,800, and I about 2,200 men, of all arms, and of these at least 5,500 are efficient....The two roads and the two positions had perhaps better be examined, I respectfully submit, before my judgement is condemned."

Wise went on to explain the merits of his position at Camp Defiance and he seemed to grow more angered as he wrote: "I am ready to join General Floyd wherever you command, and you do not say where....The enemy, while I am writing, has been firing on my pickets...I laugh him to scorn and do not stop writing, as I know he wishes to retire more now than I do....I am ready to do, suffer, and die for it, and I trust sir, that I may cite you as a chief witness of the truth of that claim...any imputation upon my motives or intentions in that respect by my superior would make me, perhaps, no longer a military subordinate of any man who breathes. I am sure you mean to cast no such imputation, whoever else may dare. I trust all will go well, most confidently, in your hands."[4]

Wise's obstinance was not repeated by anyone else, and in fact, most of the Southern troops seemed to be in awe of their new commander, as described by a member of the 22nd Virginia Infantry: "At Meadow Bluff...I saw the great Commander-in-Chief of the armies of the Confederate States of America. How distinctly I remember...the fine gray head and the kindness of his face when relaxed. It was such a face as one never forgets."[5] Another witness took no special notice of Lee's arrival, making the following entry into his diary: "Cloudy with some rain. Was relieved from guard at 8 a.m. General Robert E. Lee at Meadow Bluff and took command."[6]

Lee and Floyd spent the balance of the day inspecting the camps at Meadow Bluff and attempting to formulate a plan of action. During one of their meetings at Floyd's headquarters, a local citizen came by to complain about the troops taking the wagons and horses of local residents without paying for them. This, of course, could not be overlooked and General Floyd found it necessary to issue Special Orders #114: "Complaints have been made to General Floyd that wagons and horses have been taken from their owners for the public service and that no receipts have been given. Each QM of this brigade is ordered upon no circumstances to take private property of any kind without giving proper receipt therefor, and reporting the fact to the Col of the Rgt, who will report the same to the commanding general."[7]

Later that evening General Lee decided to accept the advice of General Wise and inspect Camp Defiance personally. The following day, the 22nd, Lee rode forward to Sewell Mountain accompanied by his 21-year-old aide, Capt. Walter H. Taylor. Taylor had been serving as Lee's only staff officer since the death of Col. John

A. Washington, at Elkwater, W.Va., on Sept. 13. A more efficient and dedicated man than Captain Taylor would have been difficult to find. Though Lee's staff reached a maximum of seven later in the war, the man who "made himself indispensable to Lee's headquarters," who "was first to last the closest," of all staff officers to Lee, was the "extremely efficient" adjutant-general, Walter H. Taylor.[8]

Upon their arrival at Camp Defiance they could hear the sounds of musket fire as another skirmish was then in progress. General Wise and several of his officers met Lee and Taylor near the headquarters tent, greeting them cordially. An officer of the 60th Virginia Infantry later recalled his first sight of Lee: "I had never seen him, and knowing our critical position I was anxious for his presence. The day of his arrival I was on the skirmish line, and it was unusually hot. I could not remain in one position as could the men, but frequently had to leave my tree...I returned to camp and saw him...there was a kindliness in his expression most unusual in one possessing eyes so dark and brilliant. He was dignified and courtly...he appeared so unconscious of his merits, so courteous, so kind, so considerate, that anyone who approached him must have felt that Lee was his very particular friend."[9]

Lee and Wise spent several hours inspecting the camps and fortifications at Sewell Mountain. Lee found the position to be a naturally strong one, as Wise had claimed, although he remained skeptical because the entire area could be flanked by a number of trails and side roads. After conferring with Wise at length, Lee left Camp Defiance without making a decision or explicitly ordering Wise to retreat.[10]

With the Federals at Camp Lookout General Cox was also active on the 22nd, ordering out additional scouting parties and notifying General Rosecrans of developments. Cox informed his commander that his scouts had reported Floyd at Meadow Bluff and Wise at Sewell, and he went on to say that the diverging roads on Sewell could be easily reached and commanded. He also told Rosecrans that he had recalled Major Hines from his advanced camp, to keep him from possibly being cut off from the brigade. General Cox had determined that he would move his entire command to Sewell on the next day, weather permitting. Rosecrans replied that the advance would be fine provided that proper precautions were taken to avoid falling into a Rebel trap. He also cautioned Cox not to advance too far, to a point where he might be compelled to fight.

That evening General Cox issued General Orders #20: "The troops will move from Camp Lookout tomorrow morning, the 23rd of September, 1861, for Big Sewell...at 8 a.m. every tent will be struck...and all fires put out. At 9 a.m. the march will be beat in the infantry and the advance sounded in the cavalry...the men will be furnished with cooked rations for two days."[11]

As the Yankees departed Camp Lookout the next morning, Cox sent a dispatch to Colonel Tyler at Gauley Bridge, advising him to keep his scouting parties "compact and watchful" and to notify him immediately of any enemy contact in his area. The brigade of General Cox advanced but three or four miles from camp when their advance guard was met along the road by a party of Confederate cavalry, under flag of truce, and commanded by Col. Nat Tyler and Maj. W. Bacon. These men had been sent out by orders of General Wise, with instructions to deliver mail to Cox's brigade from Federal prisoners that had been taken in some earlier skirmishes and at Carnifex Ferry.

Fortunately for the Yankees, their vanguard was far enough in front of the advancing army that the Rebels believed they had met only a picket guard. Had the Southerners known the full extent of the situation they could have warned their commander and possibly arranged an ambush of the Federal Brigade. Such a surprise attack would be simple to complete in the vast mountain wilderness, with its narrow winding road and numerous blind curves. As it happened, the Rebel cavalry met their adversaries near a stage stop operated by the George Masters family, and thought nothing unusual about the Yankee presence there.

Having delivered the prisoner mail, Colonel Tyler was able to garner some useful information from Cox's men, as he reported to Wise: "...I am of the opinion that Genl Rosecrans is no longer with Genl Cox...both men and officers spoke exclusively of Genl Cox command; that they were the same men who skirmished with your cavalry on the day of Floyds retreat from Dogwood Gap....An impression which dropped from an officer whom I requested to present to Genl Rosecrans my compliments for his kindness to prisoners captured at Rich Mountain, has also strengthened this opinion; he answered 'Genl Rosecrans is not here' and immediately added 'He is too far in the rear for me to see him.'[12]

No sooner had Wise's unsuspecting cavalry returned to Camp Defiance than the Yankees appeared on the western summit of Big Sewell Mountain. This sudden development managed to catch the Confederates off guard, especially so with Col. Nat Tyler who had just spoken to the boys in blue a few hours earlier, as he explained to General Lee: "I am directed by General Wise to say that the enemy in very heavy columns has occupied the top of Sewell Mountain. Infantry, cavalry, and artillery are all plainly visible from our camp, about one mile distant...they are reported by some of our cavalry as fortifying....I had just returned from the mission of truce, and the enemy came as fast as I did."[13]

Upon learning of the situation at Camp Defiance, Lee and Floyd both worried that the actual intent of the enemy was to attack Floyd's command at Meadow Bluff via the Wilderness Road. This would seem a logical conclusion as such a move would effectively flank the Wise Legion and place the Yankees well on the way to Lewisburg. With the threat of attack looming, General Floyd ordered Col. W. Ector of the 13th Georgia Infantry, to rejoin his regiment. Ector was then at a nearby residence where he had been recovering from illness acquired during his march to Meadow Bluff. Floyd explained the matter to Colonel Ector stating that, "I have this evening learned that the enemy, in considerable force, have appeared before General Wise and are engaging him. I have reason to believe that this attack is intended to hold Wise in his present position, while the much larger portion of the enemys force will advance upon me by a different road. You will therefore hasten with all dispatch to join your regiment."[14]

Floyd knew that neither his forces nor those of Wise were ready for combat, and if attack was imminent he would require every available man. In fact, the Confederates were so pitifully supplied and generally poor at this time that Floyd found it necessary to issue Special Orders #132 in an attempt to acquire horse shoes: "Any blacksmith in this camp who has the material will furnish two horse shoes and put them on the horse to be indicated by Nelson James, Wise Legion."[15]

General Lee promptly responded to Wise's dispatch advising him to carefully examine his situation and decide whether or not his force would be sufficient to withstand an enemy attack. Lee also advised Wise to "send to the rear all your incumbrances" and he told him that "the presence of the enemy before you may be a feint, to keep you in position while they advance by other roads to the rear of General Floyd." Lee was concerned that the Federals might move via Sunday Road and Nichols Mill to the Wilderness Road. Prior to writing Wise, Lee ordered Col. St. George Croghan to examine the Wilderness and Old State roads to "ascertain if there are any movements of the enemy there."[16]

Receiving Lee's dispatch after sundown, Wise responded at midnight. He told Lee that the enemy was at least 3,000 strong and stated that "I saw the masses crossing the top of Big Sewell, with artillery and cavalry. We could see about four regiments, and now count 30 camp fires....I cannot retire my baggage wagons or other incumbrances." Wise also objected to Lee's idea that the Yankees were actually advancing to Floyd's position at Meadow Bluff. He told General Lee that his cavalry had kept a frequent scout of the old road and Nichols Mill, and that there had only been a few enemy stragglers there. Wise explained the situation to his commander in a way befitting his unique character: "The idea of the enemy passing from Sunday Road to the Wilderness Road by Nichols Mill is simply absurd. There is hardly a trail there. If one, no army can possibly pass it that would startle a hare." The defiant Wise went on to say that "I am compelled to stand here and fight as long as I can endure and ammunition lasts. All is at stake with my command, and it shall be sold dearly."[17]

The rhythmic sound of a horse's hooves pounding the damp earth penetrated the haunting fog at Lee's headquarters, as a lone

Confederate courier carried Lee's reply from Meadow Bluff to Camp Defiance at 4 a.m. of Sept. 24. In his dispatch General Lee told Wise to "send word whether you have sufficient ammunition, and any information as to the operations of the enemy that may serve to regulate the movements of General Floyd." Lee also expressed his anxiety to General Wise as to the precarious situation he faced, saying, "I regret to hear that you cannot retire your baggage wagons, & etc., and are compelled to remain, as at the distance you are from support it may jeopardize the whole command."[18]

General Wise responded from Sewell Mountain at 7:15 a.m., telling Lee that "Last night in camp, very busy....I tell you emphatically, sir, that the enemy are advancing in strong force on this turnpike. They are not advancing on the old State Road at all, as yet, and none but two stragglers were seen yesterday at or near Nichols Mill....They were quiet last night, and we are ready this morning. I have a good supply of ammunition and provisions; shall keep them here, and start away my baggage wagons, if I can, this morning." Wise also told his commander about some casualties in his legion: "Their advance ceased firing at dark last evening, wounding Captain Lewis and two privates, neither mortally, though Lewis severely....If you order me to retreat, I ask that my wagons may be emptied of their baggage and the teamsters be forwarded back to me, to take off the ammunition and supplies. I desire to save everything if compelled to retire."[19]

The Captain Lewis whom Wise spoke of as wounded was 30-year-old John W. Lewis, of Company H, 59th Virginia Infantry. He soon recovered from his wounds.

Having had time to regroup his brigade, General Cox sent Rosecrans a dispatch early in the morning of Sept. 24. Cox stated that everything at his position had been quiet during the night and that he intended to scout the Rebel camps that morning. Cox obviously knew that Confederate forces were in his immediate vicinity, but he was yet uncertain whether or not they held the eastern top of Big Sewell, which of course, they did. When General Rosecrans realized that Cox had advanced his brigade to the top of

Sewell Mountain, he became concerned for the safety of the army. He told Cox, "Your position is seven miles farther in advance than I supposed....More exposed, farther from support, longer transportation, a military declaration of our intentions to use one route. Make up for these, if possible, and provide against everything."[20]

General Lee decided on the night of the 23rd to reinforce Wise at Camp Defiance, even though Lee would have preferred to unite their forces at Meadow Bluff. A careful examination of the available records reflects this opinion on the part of Lee, and it also becomes obvious that he was reluctant to order General Wise to acquiesce in General Floyd's previous orders to unite their forces in Greenbrier County. Very early on the morning of the 24th, Lee wrote to Gen. William Wing Loring, who was then encamped at Marlings Bottom or present day Marlinton, Pocahontas County. Lee ordered reinforcements from Loring, telling him, "I desire that you forward to this place such regiments as may be ready to move without delay. The enemy have advanced to Sewell Mtn in front of Genl Wise, said to be in full force, shots were exchanged last night. The road through Lewisburg is the better, the one by Frankford to the Kanawha Turnpike the shorter. By inquiry you may learn whether it will prove the speedier."[21]

Lee then asked General Floyd which regiments he could spare to accompany him as a reinforcement to Wise. Floyd selected four regiments and two pieces of artillery, consisting of the 13th Georgia, 14th North Carolina, 22nd Virginia, and 45th Virginia Infantries, and a portion of Capt. Thomas Jackson's battery of artillery. As these forces were being readied, Lee wrote Wise, saying "In ignorance of the movements of the enemy on our flanks,...I am about to advance with such portion of Genl Floyd's brigade to your support as can be spared from this position. My object is to unite the troops, I desire that you prepare your sick, baggage and whole train, with a view of retiring to this position. It is hazarding too much to remain where you are compelled to fight & have no option of withdrawing if you desire. I hope therefore you will pardon my pressing upon you the importance and necessity of making immediate arrangements for retiring you baggage & etc."[22]

The reinforcements were ordered to pack tents, baggage, and everything into wagons, and one day's rations in haversacks. After a delay of two hours the line of march was taken up at 7:00 a.m.[23]

General Floyd was left at Meadow Bluff with approximately 1,000 men, and although not all of them were now under his immediate command, he issued General Orders #27 relevant to his command structure: "This command is hereby brigaded as follows: 1st Brigade - 45th, 50th, and 51st Va Regiments - Colonel Heth 45th Regiment commanding; 2nd Brigade - 22nd and 36th Va Regiments - Colonel C.Q. Tompkins 22nd Regiment commanding; 3rd Brigade - 13th Georgia and 14th North Carolina Volunteers - Colonel W. Ector 13th Ga Infantry commanding." In organizing his artillery forces General Floyd also specified that Capt. John Henry Guy's battery be attached to the first brigade; and that the battery of Capt. Thomas Jackson be attached to the third brigade, while that of Capt. Stephen Adams, including rifled gun, be assigned to the second brigade. Brigade commanders were also ordered to submit morning reports by 10 a.m. daily.[24]

As Confederate reinforcements marched to join Wise at Camp Defiance, General Cox determined to examine the Rebel flanks, in an attempt to discover any weaknesses in their position. He ordered his artillery and several companies of skirmishers to occupy the enemy in front, while his scouts probed their defenses. At about 9:00 a.m. the Federal artillery opened fire on the Rebels as Cox's skirmishers, several hundred in number, advanced into the dark ravine separating the two camps. This sudden attack had the desired effect, in that General Wise counter-attacked in front, with strong force, not suspecting the enemies true motives. What began then as a light skirmish in the wilderness, soon evolved into more of a general engagement, several hours in duration.

A Southern officer with the 60th Virginia Infantry described the grand sight he witnessed as the Yankee attack developed: "I can never forget the advance of Rosecrans's splendid army as their bayonets flashed in the morning sun on the western summit of Sewell. Each brigade made a halt of a few minutes and then advanced to brush Wise out of the way. Wise threw forward Richardson's regiment to meet them. It was a dense forest of oaks, poplars, and chestnuts, and the regiment strung out in a picket line behind trees completely checked the advance of the enemy...it was nothing but an Indian fight--Virginians behind trees fighting Ohioans behind trees...there was no ground level enough on which to place artillery in the deep gorge between the two mountain summits."

The same writer described the weapons used by the Confederates: "We were wretchedly armed; my regiment generally had flint-lock muskets that appeared to have done service in the revolution, but perhaps half of the men had bowie-knives about 20 inches long forged in common blacksmith shops."[25]

As the skirmishing became heavy General Wise ordered out additional men, under command of Col. Charles F. Henningson, of the 59th Virginia Infantry. With Henningson were Lt. Col. Frank Anderson, Capt. Francis Imboden, and Capt. James P. Crane, with his company from the University of Virginia. Captain Crane was from Maryland and later served the Confederacy as major of the 2nd Battalion Maryland Infantry. Maj. Wade H. Gibbs commanded Wise's artillery engaged in the fight, with assistance from Capt. William McComas and Lt. Thomas Pairo.

The earth shook and the mountains echoed as bullet for bullet, and shell for shell, were released on their mission of death. As the "Indian Fighting" continued past noon, fear and anxiety were raised on both summits of Sewell, and especially at Camp Defiance, as casualty reports reached the camps. Among the Confederates, 30-year-old Lt. William Harwell and one of Captain Imboden's Louisiana Rangers were killed, and another wounded. The Rebel artillery had been placed upon a spur of the mountain, facing the Yankee camps, and as Lieutenant Pairo rode through the heavy smoke near the guns, his horse was shot from beneath him, tumbling him to the ground unmercifully, embarrassed but unhurt. Down in the ravine, closer to the scene of action, Maj. John Lawson barely escaped injury in the rugged terrain, as an enemy scout put a musket ball through his coat, and rapidly fled. On the Union side, several privates were wounded, as was Major Hines.

As General Lee and the long column of reinforcements neared Camp Defiance, they could distinctly hear the sounds of combat, and they began meeting members of the Wise Legion marching to the hospital at Meadow Bluff. Maj. Isaac Noyes Smith, of the 22nd Virginia Infantry, recorded the event in his diary: "Marching rapidly, we met men and wagons from Wise's camp at almost every turn. Many of them had great stories to tell of how the pickets were shot etc. the wagons hurrying to the rear, and we met some going rearward very rapidly whom we thought ought to be going forward." Of course the stories these men told were not without foundation, as there had been several skirmishes in the last few days, and another fight was in progress at that very time. The reinforcements pressed on, as described by Major Smith: "At the top of Sewell or near it (Mrs. Buckinghams old place) halted a moment to rest the men, had hardly sat down when the booming of cannon was heard, the Colonel jumped to his feet, called out 'forward' and we were off again."[26]

Reaching Camp Defiance around 2:00 p.m., the reinforcements were marched off into the woods and shown their place along the top of the ridge. Continual firing among the pickets echoed through the mountain defiles, and with each thunderous blast of artillery the earth shook for several yards around, causing many of the men to wonder for the first time if they would ever see the comforts of home again. Major Smith recorded his feelings in his diary: "It seems so singular that we should be here so near and for so deadly a purpose. I feel so much more like shaking them by the hand, urging them to let us alone, to go home, end this fraticidal war, and whilst they live under their government, to let us live under ours unmolested."

The fighting stopped shortly after General Lee's arrival at Sewell Mountain, and at that time General Cox sent a dispatch to Rosecrans advising him of the situation. Cox also described the Rebel position by saying that "They hold a ridge which commands the road for nearly half a mile, and have a battery of one rifled 4-pounder, one smooth sixer, and a mountain howitzer. These they used this morning....An intermediate ridge on each side, right and left, intervenes between us and them, the points of the ridges lapping by each other, and the road winds around and between them....The crest they are on is thickly wooded, and I am not yet sure whether it can be reached so as to flank them."[27]

Rosecrans responded that "You have by mistake got too near for anything but fighting unless the country between you is very forbidding. Nevertheless you will take every precaution not to be drawn into a fight....Report fully tonight on the nature of the country on your front and flanks and all the by-roads by which the enemy could surprise you." General Cox replied later that evening, telling Rosecrans: "The enemy has withdrawn the chief part of his force this evening...our rifled cannon practice was good. We dismounted their howitzer and killed a number of their cannoneers....We came here in the nick of time in my judgment, and are in no danger from their forces....On our left are long continuous ridges separated by ravines. About a mile and a half in front of our right is a bald hill, which is about the same distance from and opposite to their left....My examination of their flanks while occupying them in front has satisfied me that they are not as strong as we, except in cannon; that they were surprised by our approach; that their flanks are accessible, and that we can whip them..." [28-29]

Cox later wrote a description of the fighting in a letter to his wife: "The enemy is in plain sight, but my orders keep me from an attack until Genl Rosecrans comes up. His column has been delayed waiting for transportation. ...we had a lively skirmish, the advance guard keeping up a straggling fire three or four hours, and the enemy throwing shells and cannon balls almost constantly....We replied with a few long range shells."[30]

Maj. Rutherford B. Hayes, of the 23rd Ohio Infantry, was another witness to the fighting of Sept. 24, as he told his wife in a letter: "Firing continued...a good part of the day. Many cannon shot and shell also were let off without much result....We are ordered not to fight...until General Rosecrans arrives..."[31]

General Lee did not want to make a stand at Sewell Mountain, preferring instead the position chosen by Floyd at Meadow Bluff. It was simply Wise's obstinance and the advance of the

50

Yankees that had brought him to Camp Defiance, and he arrived in no good humor. The situation Lee found there only made matters worse. Many of the officers were discontented, ignorant of their duties, and bitter toward Floyd and his command. Lee's aide, Captain Taylor, described the situation: "The bitter feeling which had been engendered between the two commanders had imparted itself, in some degree, to the troops, and seriously threatened to impair their efficiency. No little diplomacy was required therefore, to produce harmony and hearty cooperation, where previously had prevailed discord and contention."[32]

General Lee busied himself with examining the terrain and viewing with field glasses the position held by General Cox, one mile distant. It was about this time that Lee was approached by a youthful lieutenant of a command that had been on Sewell Mountain for several days. This "green" lieutenant was T.C. Morton of the 26th Battalion Virginia Infantry, who had been directed to take a detachment and go to the ordnance train to secure what ammunition was needed for his company. The protracted rain had damaged a great deal of the ammunition carried in the soldiers cartridge boxes, and replacements were very much needed. The young officer started down the mountain with his men, and soon found himself among long lines of wagons and parks of artillery. Feeling completely lost, the party asked everyone they met, "Where is the ordnance train?" At last a soldier passing said, "Yonder is General Lee, he can tell you." The puzzled officer looked in the direction indicated and saw, not far off, a martial figure, standing in the rain by a log fire before a small tent, with his breeches tucked in his high cavalry boots, his hands behind his back, a high, broad-brimmed black hat, with a gilt cord around it, on his head, which was bowed as if in deep thought.

Writing after the war, Lieutenant Morton described his chance meeting with Lee: "The lieutenant stepped boldly up, saluted, introduced himself, and asked the general to favor him with the information as to who was the ordnance officer and where was the train? General Lee eyed his intruder a moment, and I can never forget those eyes, then said: 'I think it very strange, lieutenant, that an officer of this command, which has been here a week, should come to me, who am just arrived, to ask who his ordnance officer is, and where to find his ammunition. This is in keeping with everything else I find here, no order, no organization; nobody knows where anything is, no one understands his duty; officers and men alike are equally ignorant. This will not do.' Then pointing to a tent and some wagons on a knoll a few hundred yards off, 'There you will find what you are looking for sir, and I hope you will not have to come to me again on such an errand.'"[33]

Amid this military chaos, General Wise strode defiantly, confident his army could whip the Yankees with or without Floyd's help. In one of his brushes in thick woods, Wise ordered an artillerist to open fire. The officer protested that he could not see the enemy and could do no execution. "Damn the execution sir," Wise was reported to have said, "its the noise that we want."[34]

That night Lee bivouacked on the mountainside covered by his overcoat, for his wagon had not come up. It was about this time that he began to grow the beard that would become so familiar to Americans as the classic image of Lee. Coming to Meadow Bluff from Randolph County, he had ridden across country and had no baggage wagon when he reached Floyd; his effects did not arrive until Sept. 26.[35]

During the evening of the 24th General Floyd received some reinforcements of his own at Meadow Bluff, with the arrival of the 20th Regiment Mississippi Infantry, commanded by Col. Dan R. Russell. Floyd would later call the 20th Regiment "The flower of my command; the fine regiment from Mississippi under Colonel Russell."

Back at Sewell Mountain, two members of the 12th Ohio Volunteer Infantry left their camp, saying they were going to "view the Rebel works." This rather perilous enterprise quickly proved easier said than done, as they found it "required no small amount of labor, as we had to ford streams, traverse ravines, and ascend and descend high mountains, besides the frequent peril of discovery made a feeling of anxious suspense terribly uncomfortable, but we could not help ourselves...night was setting around us without being able to understand our whereabouts; in truth we were lost. At last it became so dark that we were oblidged to stop just at the bottom of a most frightful ravine. Thick underbrush grew all around, rendering the prospect of an attack by wild animals, or stirring up a nest of rattlesnakes, anything but pleasant."

That night a chilling rain set in and "when daylight broke the darkness, it fell upon a pair of well-nigh lifeless mortals, seated upon the bear ground, a running brook washing under us, and so nearly frozen stiff that it was with great difficulty that we arose to pursue our way." The weary Yankees did continue their mission, and early that morning reached the heights of Camp Defiance, where "suddenly we heard footsteps, and barely had time to secret ourselves, when several officers came up...apparently taking a survey of the adjacent country. The old Rebel, Henry A. Wise, was of their number, and his low tones reached our ears. We could have shot him, but to do so would have been our certain destruction." As Wise departed so did the adventurous Yankees, who eventually made their way back to their regiment.[36]

Having slept very little in his crude resting place, General Lee arose early on the morning of the 25th and summoned Captain Taylor. Lee wasted no time in attending to the business of command, especially in view of the fact that an enemy of unknown strength and intentions lie menacingly in view across the mountain gorge. So close in fact, that each day both sides could see the others waving flags and hear their drum and bugles call; as if two wings of one great army, operating in tandem.

After another careful inspection of the Yankee's encampment, Lee put down his field glasses and dictated to Captain Taylor a letter for General Floyd: "Everything is quiet in the enemy's camp. I can count five or six regiments, but cannot see ground in their rear where others may be. There is also a large wagon train for supplies...with rows of barrels piled outside...I suppose if we fall back the enemy will follow. This is a strong point, if they will fight us here. The advantage is, they can get no position for their artillery, and their men, I think, will not advance without it." Then for the first time, Lee seems to have seriously considered Camp Defiance as the point from which to make a stand. He asked Floyd "...how would it do to make a stand here?" And added "In that event we shall require provisions and forage. Of the latter there is none, and the horses are suffering...send three days rations of flour, salt, and bacon, if you have it...send also sugar and coffee..."[37]

A little later Lee ordered the 13th Regiment Georgia Infantry to entrench the large bald hill which was on their left flank, about one third mile distant. This movement was observed by General Cox, who was also active very early that morning. Cox sent General Rosecrans a dispatch informing him that the enemy still held their position, although he believed "their actions indicated a disposition to leave the Lewisburg turnpike and move toward Blue Sulphur Springs..." Also that "...there are some signs of a gun on the bald hill I mentioned, apparently with a view to protect their left flank."[38]

A few hours after sending the above dispatch to Rosecrans, General Cox ordered the 11th Ohio Infantry out on a reconnaissance to the right of the Rebels camp on Big Sewell. This regiment, commanded by Col. J. Frizell, had successfully surprised the Confederates on three other occasions, and this fact undoubtedly played a part in Cox's decision to use them, when numerous other regiments were available. In fact, the 11th Ohio Infantry had already gained a reputation as "Frizell's Gipsies" and considered themselves, the "best in the field." In writing a letter home, a member of the boasted regiment, told his family that "...we have done as much work as any regiment in Virginia, had more skirmishes, killed more Rebs, and received less newspaper praise than any other regiment...we are here, there and everywhere, and when the Rebs think they have us, we aint there...as we know all the roads, paths, houses, people, and have been over all their big hills, can sleep in logs, behind stumps, in rain or shine, can make the biggest show with the fewest men, and the biggest fight on record." (Such a modest fellow he was.)[39]

Moving through the tangled undergrowth of the dense forest, Frizell's men had not gone far when Confederate pickets opened fire. Initially, the Federals drove back the few Rebels they encountered and advanced nearer their objective. When the picket firing became general, Wise, himself, led a strong force of skirmishers out to meet the advancing enemy, and rifle fire was opened at long range. Companies A and F of the 11th Ohio were deployed in the advance, and the men fired at the Rebels whenever they could be seen through the bushes and thickets. Louis Brossy and James Mahan of Company A, 11th Ohio, soon found themselves separated from their comrades, and among the confusion and sounds of battle, unintentionally walked into Camp Defiance, and were made prisoners.

This rugged probe counter-probe skirmishing continued well into the afternoon, when, at about 4:30 p.m., a courier handed General Wise an order from Confederate President Jefferson Davis, which would permanently end the military fiasco of Wise and Floyd: "General Henry A. Wise, Sir...You are instructed to turn over all the troops heretofore under your command, to General John B. Floyd, and to report yourself in person to the Adjutant General in the city of Richmond, with the least delay...in making the transfer to General Floyd, you will include everything under your command."

Explicit as were the terms of the order, Wise debated whether to obey or defy the War Department, as he had already defied Floyd. In his hesitation he wrote General Lee, asking his opinion, and stating, in part, that "I desire to delay my report in person until after the fate of this battle. Dare I do so? On the other hand, can I, in honor, leave you at this moment, though the disobedience of the order may subject me to the severest penalties? Will you please advise and instruct me.?"[40]

One has to wonder what thoughts raced through the mind of Robert E. Lee, as he realized he may not be able to rid himself of this insolent general, even by orders from the president. Lee replied as quickly as circumstances would allow, urging Wise to comply with the order: "...appreciating, as I do, the reluctance and embarrassment you feel at leaving your Legion at this time,...I should feel...that is, to obey the President's order."[41]

Wise drafted a farewell to his men, announcing his recall and affirming that when President Davis instructed he be relieved, he could not have foreseen that the order would be received when the troops were in the face of the enemy. The old general immediately packed his baggage and left for Richmond the next morning, reaching that city on the 28th., accompanied by Colonel Henningsen, Maj. C. Duffield, Capt. E. Maury, Capt. W. Tabb, and his son, Capt. Wise.[42-43]

Gen. Robert E. Lee as he would have appeared when he arrived in Fayette County. He grew his famous gray beard while camped on Sewell Mountain. COURTESY W.VA. DEPT. OF CULTURE & HISTORY

56

VMI Cadet Walter H. Taylor in 1855 at the age of 16. During the war he became Lee's most trusted aide and remained so untiil Appomattox. After the war he wrote two books on his experiences with the Army of Northern Virginia. He died in 1916. This is a rare photo and has not been previously published in a book. COURTESY CARROLL WALKER AND JANET TAYLOR, NORFOLK, VA

Another rare view of Walter Taylor, this one taken on April 1, 1861, when Taylor was 1st Lieutenant of Company F, 6th Virginia Regiment Militia. COURTESY CARROLL WALKER AND JANET TAYLOR, NORFOLK, VA

Maj. Gen. Gabriel C. Wharton of the 51st Virginia Infantry.

Capt. Francis Imboden. He commanded a company of Louisiana Rangers at Sewell Mountain. COURTESY BILL TURNER, LAPLATA, MD

Rosecrans and Rain

A steady rain was falling on the morning of Thursday, Sept. 26, as the despondent General Wise rode away from Sewell Mountain, never to return. As it happened, Wise's departure coincided with General Rosecrans arrival at the camp of General Cox. Now, for the first time, Rosecrans viewed for himself the position held by General Lee, upon the eastern crest of Sewell. General Rosecrans found the situation at Cox's camp a poor one indeed. Many of the same problems which plagued the Confederates also existed within the Federal camps. There was a lack of discipline and a severe need for experienced officers to lead and control the "raw" troops. Though Union troops were generally better supplied, there was much waste and inefficiency occasioned by the need of experienced quartermasters. Disease was equally a problem. Hundreds of men were sick with measles, acute diarrhea, typhoid, and other ailments. Many of the homes and churches between the western top of Sewell Mountain and Gauley Bridge, a distance of about 32 miles, were used as hospitals. Food for the men and forage for the horses were rapidly becoming a problem, and the few items which were available had already seen a substantial increase in price.

Having had time to confer with his officers at Sewell, Rosecrans decided to personally conduct a reconnaissance of Lee's encampment. He took with him Generals Cox and McCook, along with Maj. Rutherford B. Hayes, and their staff officers, assisted by a company of infantry. Once near the enemy's works, the light rain suddenly became a torrential downpour, thoroughly soaking the party, and causing Major Hayes to confess that "I hardly expect to be dry again until the storm is over."

Rain or shine, the mere presence of Rosecrans, the renown victor of Rich Mountain, boosted morale among officers and men

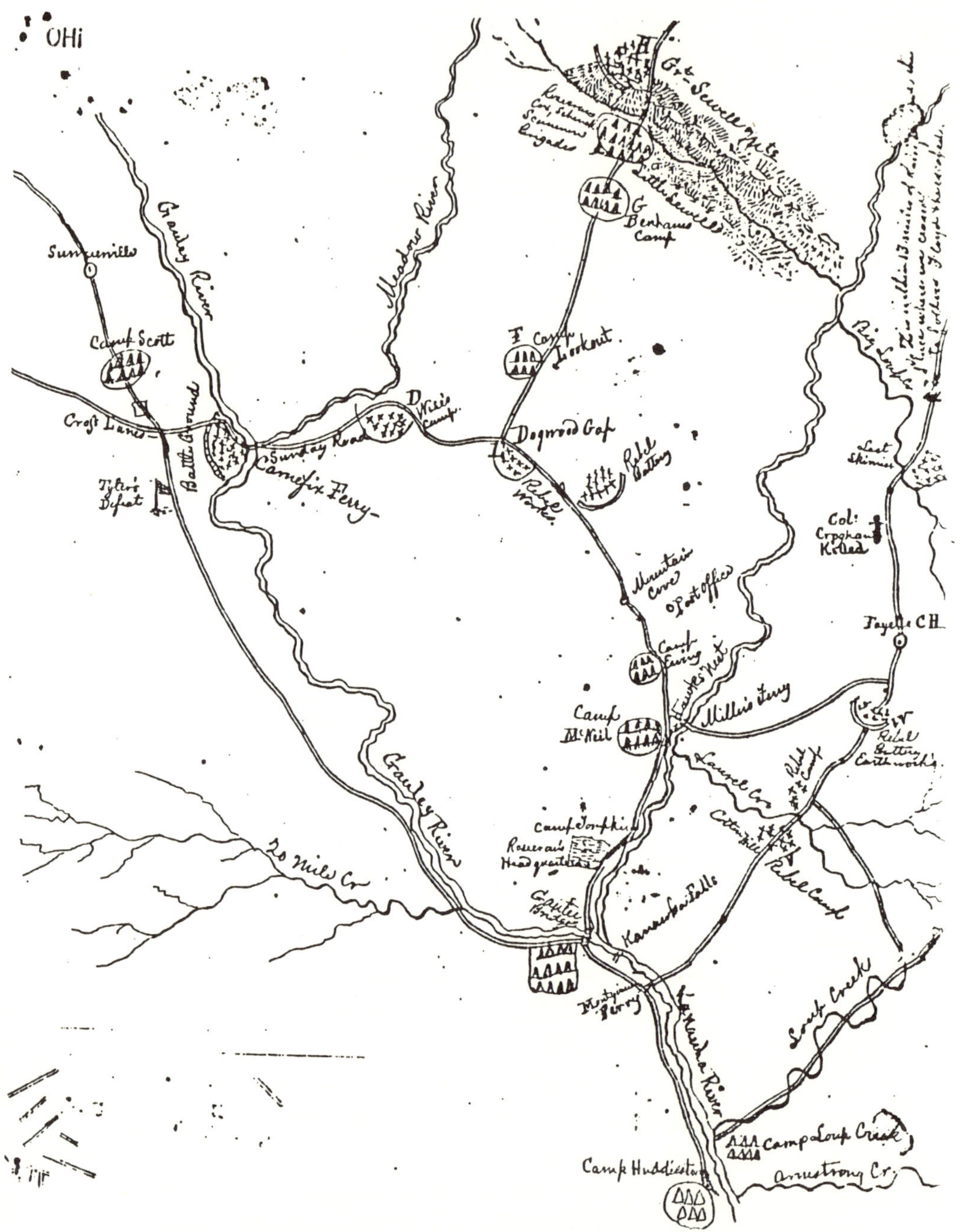

Map showing military camps between Gauley Bridge and Sewell Mountain. Drawn by R.D. VanDuerson of the 12th O.V.I.
COURTESY OHIO HISTORICAL SOCIETY

60

alike. A young officer of the 26th Ohio Infantry, wrote his father, saying that "With his presence I suppose we will again start in pursuit, that is if they will not make a stand. Lewisburg is only two days off, and the railroad 20 miles from there, and if they reach the railroad before we catch them, they will escape, if not we will get every one of them certain. If we succeed we will burn Lewisburg and stop at White Sulphur Springs awhile..."[1]

Following behind General Rosecrans, at a slower pace, was the brigade of Col. Eliakim P. Scammon, consisting of the 13th, 23rd, and 30th Ohio Regiments of Infantry. Scammon's brigade had progressed only the few miles from Camp Lookout to Locust Lane, on the 26th, and found themselves victims of the hard rain which caught Rosecrans on reconnaissance. Frank Jones, of the 13th Ohio Infantry, told his wife of the ordeal: "...a cold rain blew up and at 4 oclock in the midst of it, we received orders to march to this point, 4 miles distant, which we reached in the dark and rain and took such shelter as we could find, in a deserted cabin, where I am now writing, and its outhouses, where it has been as much as we could do to keep warm and dry..."[2]

The cold rains and strong winds that had set in would prove to be a deluge of three days duration. The inundation was complete and disastrous. Young and old alike had never witnessed such heavy and continuous rains in this region and the turnpike, which was seldom in good condition, even in dry weather, now seemed to disappear: "The roads were in a dreadful condition; the bottoms appeared to have dropped out."[3] Another witness recorded: "In some places, every trace of the road had been so completely washed away that no one would dream that any had ever been where were then gullies eight or ten or even fifteen feet deep."[4]

Disease and supply problems, which were already at near intolerable levels in both camps, became many times worse before the storms ended. The storms prompted General Floyd to tell Lee that "At this season of the year, I do not remember to have seen such a storm in the mountains of Virginia. It has put an almost absolute stop to all locomotion." A member of the 22nd Virginia Infantry made the following entry into his diary: "The rain poured on pitilessly; the poor fellows were shivering in the wet and cold. A more merciless, cheerless rain, and more miserable day could scarcely have been experienced by anyone. The poor, half frozen, half starved men had to stand it. We were all thoroughly drenched, and with difficulty kept the rain from extinguishing our fire."[5]

Despite the rains, military necessity required Blue and Gray alike to conduct at least a semblance of business as usual. At Meadow Bluff, General Floyd found it necessary to issue Special Orders #148: "Colonel A W Reynolds 50th Regiment Va Vols Floyd Brigade, will proceed at once to the Greenbrier White Sulphur and there establish and organize a general hospital for the sick of this command. Colonel Reynolds will give any order for the proper management of the hospital. He will also give strict attention to the recruiting up of his regiment, which has been much reduced by sickness."[6]

At Camp Defiance, General Lee had requested additional reinforcements, and Floyd sent him the 20th Mississippi Infantry, and one rifled cannon. With their departure Floyd's command consisted of the 36th, 50th, and 51st Virginia Infantry Regiments; about 1,000 men. The Mississippi soldiers were late in the afternoon getting started on their march, and just after dark the rain turned into sleet. Men and horses alike suffered immeasurably and progress was slow. Finally, at about 10:00 p.m., during the worst of the sleet storm, the reinforcements reached Camp Defiance. Their arrival was described by J.H. Miller: "We arrived at Big Sewell Mountain about ten oclock at night in a pelting storm of sleet, without tents, wagons, or any kind of vessel to cook in, the wagon train being left behind coming up the third day after our arrival. We could get plenty of raw rations, beef and flour, but how to cook the bread was a problem we were sometime in solving. We after many thoughts, struck the keynote by making flour in a dough, drawing it out in a long roll and wrapping it around an iron ram-rod, placing the forks near the fire and laying the ram-rod in the forks, turning the rod as necessary, you soon had a roll of bread nice enough for the lord to dine on."[7]

With the reinforcements arrival Lee informed Floyd that he

may have to order the men back to Meadow Bluff, as they had arrived without provisions and forage, and none was available at Sewell Mountain. He asked Floyd to inform him whether arrangements had been made to obtain sufficient supplies for all the troops. Lee also stated that two prisoners had been captured that day, and that they claimed the Yankee force in the area totalled 12,000. Before bedding down for the night, Lee wrote his first letter from Sewell Mountain to his wife Mary: "I have just received, dear Mary, your letters of the 17th and 19th instants, with one from Robert. I have but little time for writing tonight, and will, therefore, write to you....I infer you received my letter written before leaving Valley Mountain...I told you of the death of Colonel Washington. I grieve for his loss...It is raining heavily. The men are all exposed on the mountain, with the enemy opposite to us. We are without tents, and for two nights I have lain buttoned up in my overcoat. Today my tent came up and I am in it. Yet I fear I shall not sleep for thinking of the poor men. I wrote about socks for myself....If you can send them here, I will distribute them to the most needy...May God guard and bless you."[8]

The accommodations at General Cox's camp were no better than Lee's, and since General Rosecrans had not been able to bring up his headquarters train, he spent the next two or three days sharing a tent with Cox and Gen. Robert C. Schenck. General Cox later described the situation: "In my own tent General Rosecrans occupied my camp cot; I had improvised a rough bunk for myself on the other side of the tent, but as General Schenck got in too late for the construction of any better resting place, he was obliged to content himself with a bed made of three or four camp stools set in a row."[9]

Rain was still falling the next morning, and General Floyd received word from Colonel Croghan at White Sulphur Springs that he would attempt to forward supplies. Croghan had gone to the springs on Floyd's orders, with instructions to speed the movement of supplies from that point to Meadow Bluff. The Greenbrier River had risen so high that in many places the road had been washed away, and Colonel Croghan had to swim his horse across the river to reach White Sulphur Springs. Once there he ordered crews of men out to repair the roads, which was done in spite of the inclement weather. Later in the day Croghan was able to send General Floyd 60 barrels of flour and several barrels of pork. He had hoped to send a larger quantity of supplies but the flooding river swept away 12 barrels of flour and an entire wagon load of pork. Croghan also informed Floyd that the additional reinforcements ordered by General Lee had passed his position and encamped at Bungers Mill, four miles west of Lewisburg. These were the troops commanded by Gen. W.W. Loring and Col. William Phillips.

Floyd then notified Lee of General Loring's arrival near Lewisburg, and explained that he had sent forward that morning all provisions which wagons could be found to carry. Transportation at Floyd's camp was entirely inadequate, and the wagons which were available could only carry half-loads because mud was so thick on the turnpike that the poor horses simply could not pull the usual load. Floyd also told Lee that the swamps in his area were full beyond precedent, and that his flanks were fully secured by water against any lateral movement by the enemy. He went on to suggest that all their forces be united at Meadow Bluff: "The passage of the two Sewells and the dreadful gorge between them interposes most formidable barriers to the supply of the army, and presents, I think, a fair ground for consideration as to the task of imposing it upon the enemies instead of assuming it ourselves....Two or three weeks at least must elapse before the enemy would venture upon a flank movement...The distance from our main depot of supply (Lewisburg) just half of what it is to the top of Big Sewell. Under these circumstances I leave it to your better judgment to determine what policy is to be pursued."[10]

Lee responded by asking Floyd for additional artillery: "I find that additional cannon could be advantageously used on our left, the weakest point, where the regiments of your brigade are posted. Can you spare a section of Guy's battery? If so, please send them, with provisions and forage for three days, and two tents for the men. Tell the officer in charge to bring his ammunition - 100 rounds at least....We have had a terrible storm all day in these mountains, and I fear the men have suffered much..."[11] To which Floyd responded that he would start "immediately additional provisions for the troops, and shall use every possible effort to keep them supplied. The country hereabouts is inundated by the rain...still, every human effort shall be made in this direction."[12]

A Confederate officer at Camp Defiance later recalled that "The rain was daily falling in torrents, and by that time at such an altitude it was very cold. The roads were not macadamized and almost impassable...the men were becoming anxious for a fight. The greater part of them never having seen any thing more alarming that the daily skirmishing in which we were engaged, really believed each one the equal of five Federals."[13] From the opposite crest of Sewell, Rutherford Hayes wrote his wife, saying that "We are in the midst of a very cold rain-storm...rain for fifteen hours; getting colder and colder, and still raining. In leaky tents, with wornout blankets, insufficient socks and shoes, many without overcoats. This is no joke."[14]

It certainly was not a joke, it was war, and as the rains subsided a little that evening an incident occurred which reminded everyone of that fact. Lt. Col. James W. Spalding, of the 60th Regiment Virginia Infantry, suddenly and unexpectedly decided to conduct an advanced scout of the enemy. This scout was totally unauthorized and it was reported that Spalding had been drinking, and in fact, was intoxicated. Ordering out one of his companies, he advanced beyond the Rebel pickets who were posted just 300 yards from the enemy. Carelessly, he rode out in advance of his escort and soon found himself face to face with the pickets of the 30th Ohio Infantry, recently arrived. Gen. Hugh B. Ewing, of the 30th Ohio, described the event in a letter to his wife: "Colonel Spalding rode up the mountain, turned the curve, and suddenly came upon the picket. He reined his horse, drew his pistol and fired, they fired, he missed them, they shot him in the breast. His horse whirled and ran down the mountain, carrying him fifty yards and hurling him to earth in the midst of his escort. They fled carrying off his body. He left at the spot where he fell, a pool of blood, his pocket book and papers, fallen from his breast pocket. All cut by bullets or stained by his hearts blood."[15]

Another Federal witness told his wife that "he came upon our pickets, perhaps without knowing it & drew his pistol...they immediately leveled their guns & fired. He fell forward on his horse as it bore him away, but there fell from his breast pocket, the miniature of his wife & a packet of papers. On the back of the picture was written 'Seperated by this cruel and unnatural war.' The lady is in Pittsburg, the husband killed."[16]

Maj. Rutherford Hayes very succinctly offered his opinion about the event: "Our pickets killed a colonel or lieutenant colonel of the enemy who rode among them. All wrong and cruel. This is too like murder."[17]

Word of Spalding's death rapidly spread among the camps, and one man noted that "at a branch I saw a negro boy washing blood from a saddle and was told a few moments before Colonel Spalding was shot by the Yankee pickets and the warm blood still on his saddle. It made me feel sad but I soon heard it was his own rashness in going against General Lee's order while drunk. He was much beloved, but was much in the habit of drinking."

Spalding thus became the second Confederate officer killed at Sewell Mountain, and the third killed in Fayette County. His sudden and shocking death was a severe blow to morale among the Southern troops, especially in his own regiment.

That night the cold rains continued with many men in Blue and Gray lying unprotected, fully exposed to the elements. These severe hardships at Sewell Mountain were not easily forgotten by the troops, and many of them who went on to serve in grandiose and sanguinary campaigns of the war, would later recall first the privations experienced in the West Virginia wilderness. General Rosecrans recalled, several years later, that while he was at Sewell: "One of the most terrible storms ever known set in. Eighteen horses perished in one night at headquarters....The roads became almost impassable."[18]

Early the next morning, the 28th, the rain was still pouring and General Floyd wrote to Lee to advise him that high waters had damaged the roads and bridges, delaying the supply train: "I understand that the bridges have been carried off in two places between

66

this camp and Sewell, which may delay the transportation of supplies until they can be repaired. The streams are still very high but are rapidly subsiding. They shall be crossed and provisions sent forward as soon as this is possible."[19]

Of course in spite of the bad weather the men had to eat, and down in the great ravine separating the two armies, a sort of military "cat and mouse" was being played out for food. A member of the 12th Ohio Infantry, who had been among the pickets at Sewell Mountain, later recalled that "the chief incentive for fighting was a herd of fine cattle which both sides wanted. Every day small bodies of men would make a dash to capture a fine beef, and while part of them drove away the rebel guards, the others made off with the prize. Singular as it may seem, in all these skirmish engagements not a man lost his life, and but one case of wounding occured. On the rebel side, the mortality was known to be large."[20]

At Camp Defiance officers of the 60th Virginia Infantry petitioned Lee for a replacement to Colonel Spalding. Capt. Alexis Buster, as senior captain, was chosen and served a few days as commander of the regiment, until Col. William E. Starke was appointed.

That afternoon some of the supplies sent by Colonel Croghan reached Meadow Bluff, and Croghan explained that he had discovered the delay in moving supplies to Camp Defiance was due to an earlier order from General Wise, that no additional provisions be sent. Apparently, Wise had failed to rescind his order of Sept. 18, and also had not informed Lee or Floyd of its existence. Accordingly, provisions had not been forwarded to Sewell Mountain for eight days by the time Colonel Croghan discovered the problem and revoked the order. This, of course, was poor management on Wise's part, and his mistake was further compounded by the fact that 50 wagons used to transport supplies had been kept at Sewell, instead of being returned to the depot as usual.

Attempting to get the Confederate supply system functioning properly was difficult enough, without such errors, and Croghan was several days at White Sulphur Springs supervising the shipments. He informed Floyd on the 28th that he was sending five boxes of overcoats, 400 rounds of cannon ammunition, and 50,000 rounds of small arms cartridges. Also that work was still underway on the turnpike, and that he would speed the transportation system generally, when the repair was complete.[21]

With the inclement weather there naturally came a lull in skirmishing, and it was not uncommon for Blue and Gray pickets at Sewell to exchange Kanawha salt for Greenbrier beef. They would also discuss the merits of each government's position in the conflict. While the majority of Yankees at Sewell were from Ohio, some had been residents of the Kanawha Valley who had enlisted into Ohio regiments.

The severe weather also kept General Lee near his tent, and he spent many hours in conference with his commanders, and entertaining occasional guests. Lee's aide, Captain Taylor, later wrote a description of the headquarters on Big Sewell Mountain: "One solitary tent constituted his headquarters camp; this served for the general and his aide; and when visitors were entertained, as actually occured, the general shared his blankets with his aide, turning over those of the latter to his guest. His dinner service was of tin, tin plates, tin cups, tin bowls, everything of tin, and consequently indestructible; and to the annoyance and disgust of the subordinates, who sighed for porcelain, could not or would not be lost."[22]

At five p.m. of the 28th Phillips Legion of Georgia Cavalry and Riflemen arrived at Meadow Bluff, on their way to join Lee. This swelled the Confederate force there by approximately 400 men. At six p.m. of the same day, Gen. William Wing Loring arrived at Floyd's camp, bringing two regiments and a battery of artillery. Following behind Loring by about one-half day's march, was Gen. Samuel Read Anderson, with the 1st, 7th, and 16th Regiments Tennessee Infantry. Loring had brought the 42nd and 48th Regiments Virginia Infantry.

General Anderson was 57 years old, and was a veteran of the Mexican War. General Loring, in command of all five regiments, was 42 years old and also a veteran of the Mexican War, having lost his left arm in the fighting at Mexico City.

Their march to reinforce General Lee had been an arduous one indeed. They had traveled on foot from Big Spring, near present-day Slatyfork, and from present-day Marlinton, Randolph County, to Meadow Bluff. A distance of approximately 80 miles. The creeks and streams, which they had to ford, were swollen completely out of their banks and looked more like rivers.

Richard N. Hewitt, of the 42nd Virginia Infantry, told his wife that "I have waded mud and given brandy & quinine along the train of wagons till I could barely travel...but be of good cheer for God will yet deliver us from this earthly hell. You have no idea of the trials we undergo. The rain has been constant & the mud knee deep & the horses broken down & the officers & men disheartened...we had to march day & night & carry the sick in wagons & you never saw such work."[23]

UNION ARMY ROLL-CALLS
HOURS AND ORDER OF SERVICE
SEWELL MOUNTAIN, VA 1861

Three roll-calls daily: **Reveille, Retreat** and **Tattoo**

Reveille: 5:30 a.m. - All quarters put in order

Squad drills at 30 minutes after Reveille, for one hour

Peas-upon-a-trencher: Signal for breakfast, two hours after Reveille

Troop: Signal for guard mounting, three hours after Reveille; Morning Reports filed at this time

Surgeon's Call: Four and one-half hours after Reveille

Roast Beef: Signal for dinner at 12 noon

<u>**The Assembly**</u>**:** Signal to form by company and drill for one hour; sounded at 3:00 p.m.

<u>**Retreat**</u>**:** Companies assembled for inspection and released for supper; sounded at 4:30 p.m.

<u>**Tattoo**</u>**:** No soldier out of their tent or quarters unless on leave or special duty. Sounded at 9:00 p.m.

<u>**Taps**</u>**:** All lights extinguished; sounded at 9:30 p.m.

UNION ARMY GUARD DUTY
CONDUCTED UNDER THREE DESIGNATIONS

First: <u>Brigade Guard</u> - directed by Field Officer of the day. Responsible for establishing Sentinels around entire encampment

Second: <u>Police Guard</u> - All sanitary matters, and matters affecting the order and discipline of the camp

Third: <u>Quarter Guard</u> - Responsible for the discipline, order and sanitary conditions of their respective quarters

Gen. William Wing Loring. He brought reinforcements to General Lee at Camp Defiance. AUTHOR'S COLLECTION

Charles S. Powell, Co. E, 14th North Carolina Infantry. Disease reduced his regiment from 750 to just 277 men fit for duty during the Sewell Mountain campaign. COURTESY WILLIAM S. POWELL

Scouts on Sewell Mountain, 1861. COURTESY FAYETTE COUNTY HIS-
TORICAL SOCIETY

72

Printed by Ehrgott, Forbriger & Co. Cincinnati.
STORM.
(Mountain)
(ance)

Pvt. Thomas D. Gooch of the 20th Mississippi Infantry. Over 60 percent of his regiment became ill at Sewell Mountain due to heavy rains and cold weather. COURTESY MUSEUM OF THE CONFEDERACY

Poised to Strike

On Sunday the 29th, everyone breathed a sigh of relief as the rains had ceased and the sun was once again visible in a clear blue sky. The troops were encouraged to attend church services, which were held in several areas of the camps. Having the Sabbath day to rest and forage, the men welcomed the opportunity to mingle with their friends and write letters to their loved ones. Some of the men struck out on their own in search of food. One such search involved General Lee and his staff, as described by Pvt. Leroy W. Cox:

At one time a bridge washed away, which cut us off from all supplies. For three days we had no rations. One day Bill Catterton, a young fellow by the name Dodd, and myself, got permission to go out and hunt for something to eat, that is, to buy something if we could find anything to buy. We called it a pirating expidetion. We finally came across one of our headquarters wagons and bartered with the fellow in charge of it for about a quart of flour. He said we could have it for fifty cents. We had no change, nothing but a five dollar Confederate bill among us and he couldnt make change. Bill Catterton, an illiterate mountaineer and a tremendous giant of a man, said, "Here, give me the bill, I'll get it changed." It happened that General Lee was standing nearby and Catterton went straight up to him, addressing him thus, "How do you do, General?" and put out his hand to shake hands with him. I can see that ugly hand now as he offered it to the General. It had one time been mangled by a hog and was terribly disfigured. "How are you, General, and hows your family?" "All well the last time I heard from them," replied the General pleasantly, as he clasped the mountaineers huge misshapen hand. "General, will you please to give me change for a five dollar bill?" The General searched in his pockets and said, "I'm sorry, I havent got it. Maybe one of these other gentlemen could give it to you." He referred to some of his staff officials who were close at hand. They all began going through their pockets and one of them announced that he had it. In the meantime, Dodd and I had stayed back at a respectful distance, viewing with horror this audacity on the part of our rough friend. However, thanks to his very audacity, we were soon in possession of the flour.[1]

Over in the Federal camp, Major Hayes penned a letter to his wife: "A beautiful bright Sunday morning after a cold, bitter, dismal storm of three days...We are compelled now by roads and climate to stop and return to the region of navigable waters or railroads. No teams can supply us here much longer. In this state of things we shall probably be content with holding the strong points already taken without fighting for more until another campaign."[2]

Hayes' feeling that the campaign at Sewell was nearing an end was also reflected by a correspondent of the <u>Wheeling Intelligencer</u>, who had visited the military hospitals operated by the Yankees, and found things in a deplorable condition: "While at Gauley Bridge, Surgeon Menzies took me to visit the hospitals at that place, and I must here confess that I never felt so much shocked in all my life, for there were men in the last agonies, suffering from cold and exposure. They had no blankets when I arrived there, but Dr. Menzies rode back to the quartermaster...and with difficulty obtained one hundred blankets to protect from the inclemency of the weather, two hundred men...the floors, walls, beds and clothing in these hospitals present a most terrible and disgusting sight from the vermin, which can be seen crawling and creeping along the whole place..."[3]

76

Despite the poor condition of the troops and the turnpike, General Rosecrans received reinforcements at 1:00 p.m. of the 29th, with the arrival of the 13th, 23rd and 30th Regiments Ohio Infantry, commanded by General Ewing and Colonel Scammon. These troops had left Camp Locust Lane at 7:00 a.m. that day and marched the 10 miles to Big Sewell Mountain in six hours. General Ewing was happy to join his commander "at the front" and recorded in his diary that on Sewell he found the "Best spring in Virginia," also that "General Rosecrans appeared very glad to see me - invited me to join him on reconnaissance. General impression - Lee here, say 1-1/2 miles off..."[4]

General Lee also received reinforcements that day, with the arrival of the 42nd and 48th Regiments Virginia Infantry, commanded by General Loring, and the two guns of Captain Guy's artillery battery which Lee had requested on the 27th, in an attempt to strengthen his left flank. With the reinforcements came additional supply problems, and General Lee wrote Floyd, telling him that "The concentration of so large a force will require great energy in the quartermasters and commissary departments. Fifty barrels of flour will be required daily for one item, and provender for the animals." With the added manpower and improved weather, General Lee focused his attention on attacking the enemy, if they did not soon attack him in his entrenched position. He told Floyd that he hoped to make an attack, saying, "General Loring informs me that you propose bringing 2,000 men yourself tomorrow. I shall be happy to see you, and if the troops are prepared with supplies for a forward movement we might drive the enemy over the Gauley. We have been threatened with an attack every day, but it has yet been suspended."[5]

If Rosecrans did not assume the offensive, the Confederates could do so by several routes to the rear of Rosecrans position. Obviously, in a country that presented such formidable natural barriers, it was far better to meet an attack than to deliver one. Of course General Rosecrans had similar ideas, preferring to meet the attack of Lee. Both sides contented themselves in scouting and fortifying, and caring as best they could for their sick. In fact,

Rosecrans' army had been reduced by disease from approximately 8,000 to just 5,200 effective.[6]

Late that evening more reinforcements reached Camp Defiance with the arrival of the 1st, 7th, and 16th Regiments Tennessee Infantry, under General Anderson. Capt. J.J. Womack, of Company E, 16th Tennessee Infantry, recorded their arrival in his diary: "We continued our march today to the top of Sewell Mountain. We had to cross two small streams today, which, from the rain on Friday, were spread our near a half mile in width, and which the soldiers had to wade, causing it to be late at night when we arrived...here, on the top of this lofty summit we pitched our camps, only one thousand yards from the enemy."[7]

Another member of the same Tennessee regiment described their arrival and the events of Monday morning, Sept. 30: "Our regiment was ordered to take a position on the right wing which we did that night, upon a long high ridge partly fortified. When morning came...there they were, commanded by their boasted Rosecrans...and stretched far and wide upon a mountain chain...their banners flying in the air amid a flourish of trumpets and martial music. Our army had a splendid position...stretched out for two miles along a high commanding ridge...the left being occupied by Floyd's Legion, the right center by Wise's Legion, and the Tennessee troops with a strong force in reserve to the rear of the center."[8]

Monday was a clear and pleasant day. A rare occurrence in these rough mountains. The Southern troops marveled at the sight of Lee and Taylor, as they clambered far up over crags and exposed rocks, daily poking about for a means of hitting at the enemy. Lee knew that attack in these hills, with their steep slopes and blind flanks, would be perilous indeed. Still, he spoiled for a fight. But there were several signs that Rosecrans was pulling his forces together for an assault, and Lee waited. His patience was severely tested as the days went by and no attack came. He wrote Floyd, saying that "I begin to fear the enemy will not attack us. We shall therefore have to attack him."[9]

The force at Lee's command continued to grow as Floyd sent up 1,700 more men and two batteries of artillery. The James River and Kanawha Turnpike was still in a terrible condition, so the men advanced along the old State Road. General Floyd had crews of men working hard to repair the roads and keep them passable, but the struggle was a huge one. He told Lee that he was again repairing the old State Road, and said that "it will be the better road for intercommunication between this point and your camp. The turnpike is almost impassable in cause, General, of the mud at certain points, and the amount of transportation over it in the last few days."[10]

When Lee had arrived at Camp Defiance he found the state of the army there to be ludicrous. He had brought up with him from Meadow Bluff, Col. Henry Heth, of the 45th Virginia Infantry, commander of Floyd's 1st Brigade. Heth's patience, like Lee's, was wearing thin. He wrote Captain Peters, Floyd's assistant adjutant general, telling him of the sorry state of things at Sewell Mountain. Heth asked Peters to inform General Floyd that since his arrival there on the 24th, "we have been without a surgeon...no commissary - no quartermaster - no doctor!" As if that were not bad enough Heth's staff officers had been absenting themselves from camp and duty without authority. He told Peters to "please start them from their comfortable retreats, as the STORM IS NOW OVER, and it is possible that they can venture out."[11]

Most of the men had not been as fortunate as Heth's staff and the rigors of duty had taken their toll. Typhoid and measles raged in the camps. Richard N. Hewitt, the 34-year-old assistant surgeon of the 42nd Virginia Infantry, told his wife that his duties and separation from her had been "the sorest trial of my life." Also that "...I pray God may preserve us to meet again in health and peace...I am compelled to be away." He explained to his wife the numerous hardships which they had to endure, and told her that he felt "just like writing a love letter." Admonishing her not to laugh, he said: "Your words of love and affection for me my darling sink deep in my heart and shall never be forgotten. Every day I live I love you more...your energy and good sense with your noble heart and mind, would make you a prize to any man in the world...the sun is down and no fight today; Good bye my love."[12]

In another section of the camp Captain Womack, of the 16th

Tennessee, relaxed in his tent and wrote of the day's activities: "We kept closely about our fires today watching the movements of the enemy & resting our weary limbs and worn out feet. We have now been without tents, and nearly without blankets, since the 8th instant; and although we have needed them very much in that time, on no occasion have we felt their absence so sensibly as here, where the constant cutting winds sweep incessantly across the towering point."[13]

There would be little sleep that night as both armies expected the other to attack. Tensions ran high on both peaks of Sewell, especially at night, when every shadow and every odd sound was thought to be the approach of the enemy. Several pickets on both sides had been killed or wounded by their own men, who had mistaken them for the enemy in the mountain darkness. Dread and suspicion filled the air and a nervous energy permeated the camps. Over 16,000 troops were now assembled in the wilderness, each awaiting the others attack. Each night General Lee had his baggage wagons and non-essential supplies moved back out of the way. The men waited and worried, they could not remain long, poised to strike. Something had to be done.

Oct. 1 dawned clear and pleasant. The third straight day of good weather and the longest break from the rains which the men would experience during this onerous campaign. Rosecrans' commanders had begun to have doubts as to the wisdom of remaining much longer in their present position. Many of them expressed a strong desire to fall back on their supply base at Gauley Bridge. Rosecrans was against a move back and counseled patience. The hours passed. The men waited and the teamsters worked. Every available wagon was put in use hauling supplies over the sodden roads. Even the headquarters baggage wagons and the regimental wagons of the troops, as well as those stationed in the rear, were pressed into service. Only half loads could be hauled. By Oct. 1, the Federals had demonstrated the fact that it was impossible to sustain their army any further from its base unless they could rely upon settled weather and good roads.

An article appeared in the <u>Cincinnati Daily Enquirer</u> criticizing General Rosecrans for his lack of a decisive victory in the mountains: "The inspiring vision of advance through Western Virginia on Staunton, and down to Richmond; or of advance to Cumberland Gap, seizure of the Tennessee and Lynchburg Railroad...all fade away before the dull reality that the roads are becoming impassable, and that General Rosecrans and his subordinates, instead of meditating bold movements to warmer climates, are already talking of hunting up winter quarters in the neighborhood of Charleston."[14]

General Lee also came under attack in the press, and among some of the men. A witness wrote of the situation: "We sat there in the mud and many of the men murmered at the masterly inactivity of Lee. Much of the press of Virginia and the South finally attacked his fabian policy, and the denunciation became general. ...My quarters being within fifty yards of Lee's tent I had a good opportunity to study him. When the daily mail came I would pass and repass his quarters to see the effect of the press and the public clamor against him. He would frequently set for an hour in the cold autumn sun on a large log near his tent reading the newspapers. I never observed the least change in his appearance. He was ever the same, quiet, self-possessed gentleman. Never a murmur escaped his lips, as I have often been informed by those who were near him."[15]

It was certainly a curious thing that both armies had among them newspaper reporters. In Richmond, all the papers were reporting in detail the plans and troop strength of Lee's army. Obviously, such a weird state of affairs could only prove detrimental to military success, yet this practice was repeated in the North. Officers and men alike frequently wrote the editors of their home-town papers, giving their impression of events in detail. These letters were however, seldom signed. Usually they would carry initials only, or a sobriquet would be used.

An example of this was an article which appeared in the <u>Richmond Enquirer</u> on Oct. 1 critical of General Floyd. It included letters written by some officers of the Wise Legion, or so it was stated, though no signatures were published. This infuriated General Floyd and he wrote the editors asking for the names of those officers, so that, "they may be tried by the military tribunals, and punished according to the laws of the army." Floyd said the Wise Legion officers had made "statements which are calumniatory falsehoods, having no shadow of truth for their foundation..."

The editors, among whom was a relative of General Wise, refused Floyd's request, or demand, telling him that they did "Not recognize any authority in yourself, either individually or as commander of the army of the Kanawha, to demand the names of our correspondents, we decline to comply with your request." The editors explained to their readers that they declined the request because Floyd intended to "seek his vindication through a court-martial instead of the usual mode among gentlemen." They then dismissed the matter, saying that "the characters of our correspondents have never been stained by the suspicion of a crime...they are gentlemen, the equals to Gen. Floyd in every respect."

General Floyd arrived in person at Camp Defiance on Oct. 1, leaving Col. James Lucious Davis in charge of Camp Meadow Bluff. The force now under Lee's command was approximately 9,000 troops, and as many as 20 cannon.[16] With this strong force the men knew something would have to be done and done soon. Maj. Isaac Noyes Smith described the emotion of the situation in his diary: "I am afraid continually that I shall never see the loved ones at home again. If we attack the enemy there will be terrible slaughter. Why should I again survive when so many are certain to be lost? How little we thought when I left the house on Monday evening that it was our last meeting for so long a time, and very possibly forever. I dread an action more on this account than any other. Floyd's troops have joined us here."[17]

In all the hardship and worry there were a few playful moments at Sewell Mountain. Henry Hutchison, of Company C 60th Virginia Infantry, possessed a habit which offended his comrades, as told by W.H. Adams: "On Big Sewell, because Hutchinson would put on a pair of old leather boots and never take them off until they were worn out, thus offending the nasal glands of everyone, we caught and threw him down, some pulling at his feet and others pulling at his head and arms, and fearing that we might pull him in

82

two, we split the boots from top to bottom, and skinned them off. Hutchison was a very big mouthed and heavy voiced man, and there and then he broke the record for swearing."[18]

The cold rain returned on Oct. 2, further demoralizing the troops. The poor men laid in their camps and many wrote letters home to their families detailing their ordeal. The three days of good weather had failed to bring on an enemy attack and many wondered how long they would suffer exposed in this mountain region. A member of the 14th North Carolina would later recall that "A great epidemic of sickness broke out among us and nearly everyone was taken sick...the regiment of over one thousand men, only stacked 56 guns at one time...many died in their tents and were buried on the road side."[19]

Thomas L. Broun, of the Wise Legion, told his wife Annie that, "For three nights in succession I slept outdoors on the cold ground, with only a counterpane to protect me from the mountain winds. The whole regiment, except two or three persons, did the same thing, expecting an attack every night from the Yankees. It was too much for me, as well as many others. Consequently I was made very sick. Had a bad diarrhea, fever, head-ache and pains through all my limbs. I am confined sick I have been for a week."[20]

Despite the rains General Lee hoped to drive the Yankees from Western Virginia. Unlike so many others he had not yet lost hope that a victory could be had before winter. Lee kept diligent rein over military matters at Sewell and waited for Rosecrans' attack, which he felt certain would come. He had by this time assembled sufficient ammunition, supplies, and manpower, to expect a victory, though Lee well understood that there were constraints of time as winter rapidly approached. William A. Jackson, ordnance officer of the Wise Legion, sent Lee an inventory of ammunition on hand:

To Genl R.E. Lee
Camp Defiance
Oct 2 1861

Report of ammunition in hands of ordnance officer at

this encampment.

> 98,000 musket (flint) cartridges
> 16,000 ball & buckshot musket cartridges with caps
> 7,000 Harpers Ferry Rifle Cartridges with caps
> 4 Kegs rifle powder
> 2 Kegs 100 H Lead
> 31,500 Musket Percussion caps
> 5,000 Shotgun & pistol or Country Rifle caps
> 4,000 Navy pistol (Colts) cartridges & caps
> 1,000 Army pistol rounds & etc[21]

There was no attack on the night of the 2nd, and the next morning Maj. Rutherford Hayes penned a letter to his wife: "This is a pleasant morning...We are evidently at the end of our campaign in this direction for this season...I think there will be no battle here. The enemy are strongly entrenched and far superior to us in number...They have twenty-two pieces of artillery."[22]

General Rosecrans had not yet given up on the campaign and he ordered Col. R.S. McCook to send out a strong scouting party with instructions to capture a Confederate cavalry picket, and to "examine the road well up towards the Rebels."[23] Like Lee, Rosecrans was daily probing, peering, and waiting. There had been skirmishes daily for two weeks, but no pitched battle, only a war of nerves. A skirmishing war that prompted an officer of the 23rd Ohio Infantry to comment on Oct. 3 that "This whistling of projectiles about one's ears is disagreeable. It made me try to think of all my old prayers; but I could only remember, 'Oh Lord, for these and all thy other mercies, we desire to be thankful."

The weather was cloudy and warm on the 3rd, and there seemed to be increased activity in the Yankee camps. General Lee viewed the movements with his field glasses and believed an attack was imminent. There had been considerable noise from the movement of wagons and artillery on the day before, and if Rosecrans did not attack soon, Lee would. During the afternoon Lee had all the wagons loaded and sent to the rear, and the men were told to prepare for a march with no specific reason given. Understandably, these events caused great anxiety within the camps and the men hoped for a defensive rather than offensive action.

Additional Confederate pickets were posted to alarm the camp if the enemy advanced, and at 8 p.m. General Lee issued orders to prepare for action. The order read in part: "The commanding officers of brigades & corps will cause their several commands to be inspected this evening & will see that their arms and ammunition of their men are in perfect order for service. They will also see that all their effective force are at their posts."[24]

Word of the order spread quickly among the troops, as recalled by Marcus Toney, of the 1st Regiment Tennessee Infantry, "On the night of October 3rd we received orders to have our guns cleaned and in shape for the following morning...our information was that they were to attack us early the next morning...we were ready to meet the enemy."[25]

With the situation as it was, there would be little sleep. Major Smith described the pre-dawn events of Oct. 4: "At quarter past three oclock we were all up, and ready very shortly after to receive the enemy. Every moment we awaited the opening of the enemys guns, and so continued until late in the day. At twelve oclock I thought it more than probable no attack would be made during the day. You have no idea of the excitement such a state of things produces, but I have been so long accustomed to such things that the effect is nothing like it would be to inexperienced persons."[26]

Lee remained convinced that an attack was imminent. All day he had the men constructing additional breastworks and fortifying. The weather was clear and pleasant. The sounds of trees being felled for breastworks was several times met with the echo of musket fire from the pickets. Nine thousand Confederate soldiers remained on alert; waiting and listening. Some praying, some writing letters, and others convinced there would be no fight. One man wrote that Oct. 4 went so slowly it "seemed like two days." It certainly must have felt that way to Lee and his officers as they hoped to meet the Yankees on their terms, at Camp Defiance.

There would be no battle. The Union soldiers held their

positions; defiant and menacing. At noon Capt. J. Hudson and 40 men of Company C, 10th Ohio Infantry, were sent out on yet another Federal reconnaissance. They took a detour of several miles around the Confederate left flank and came upon the rear of Lee's lingering army. Captain Hudson and his intrepid cohorts crept stealthily along the mountain ridges and slopes, peering and peeking at their unsuspecting hosts. Moving quietly through tangled thickets and open woods, from boulders to logs, they soon accomplished their mission, and "then laid in the wilderness until dusk, when, according to orders, made the best of his way back to headquarters."[27]

Captain Hudson reported that he found a "series of formidable earthworks, and a line of camps extending a distance of about five miles." This report seemed to confirm General Rosecrans suspicion that Lee's army vastly outnumbered his own. Already, Rosecrans had been given estimates from his scouts of as many as 30,000 Rebels in his front. This of course caused a great timidity on the Federal part, when in actuality Lee's army was nearly identical in numbers to the Federals.

It seems that Rosecrans and his officers failed to consider terrain as the reason why Lee's camps extended a distance of several miles. They were spread out, not because of numbers, but due instead to the broken terrain and dense wilderness. The Sewell Mountain range is made up of a series of narrow ridges and protruding peaks or knobs. Each ridge has a corresponding ravine, some shallow, some dark and deep. A very difficult region in which to move an army for defense or offense.

General Rosecrans entered the campaign with approximately 8,200 men of all arms. General Lee had assembled, by Oct. 1, approximately 9,000 men. Depending upon the numbers of men too sick for duty at any given time, we can see that no advantage of numbers existed for either side, sufficient to turn the tide of battle in their favor. It was thus two nearly identical armies that had lain and looked at each other for a fortnight.

Col. R.B. Snowden, commander of the 1st Regiment Tennessee Infantry.

Maj. Joseph Vaulx, of the 1st Tennessee Infantry. He was among the brave foot soldiers of Tennessee who fought at Camp Defiance.

Dr. J.P. Hanner, 1st Regiment Tennessee Infantry. He helped care for the hundreds of men who became sick at Camp Defiance.

Dr. J. Robinson Buist, assistant surgeon of the 1st Tennessee Infantry at Camp Defiance.

Pvt. Robert Cheatham of the 1st Tennessee Infantry. A boy of 17 while at Sewell Mountain.

Pvt. Samuel D. Morgan of the 1st Tennessee Infantry. A boy of 19 at Sewell Mountain, he was killed in Kentucky in 1862.

Capt. W.N. Tate of the 7th Tennessee Infantry.

Col. John Savage of the 16th Tennessee Infantry. Commander of Lee's right flank at Sewell Mountain.

Flight of the Yankees

Oct. 5 was a calm, sunny day and it was spent the same as the preceding day, in hourly expectation of a fight. Having some spare time to do as they pleased, two members of the 46th Virginia Infantry climbed to a prominent point on the mountain from which they could view the Yankee camp. They had not been there long when visitors arrived: "Who should come walking up while we were there but General Lee and General Loring. They had a pair of field glasses and had come to view the Union troops. On their arrival we withdrew to a little distance in order that they might have the advantage of the best point. After they looked at the troops with their field glasses for some moments, General Lee tendered them to my brother saying, `Wouldn't you like to look at them?' When he returned them, the general also handed them to me. I was delighted at his thoughtfulness for even a mere boy like myself."[1]

What the Confederates could not have known was that General Rosecrans had already decided to retreat and had made preparations to slip away in the night. General Cox described the movement: "During the fifth of October our sick and spare baggage were sent back to the Camp Lookout. Tents were stuck at ten o'clock in the evening, and the trains were sent on their way under escort at eleven...my own brigade was assigned rear guard. We remained upon the crest of the hill until half past one, the men being formed in line of battle and directed to lie down until time for them to march...The troops had marched but a mile or two when they overtook part of the wagon train toiling over the steep and slippery hills. Here and there a team would be stalled in the mud...When at last day broke, we were only three or four miles from our camp of the evening before...the men broiled their coffee, cooked their breakfast, and rested."[2]

A member of the 11th Ohio Infantry remembered of the difficult night march that "...we did not get off till morning of the

6th...Through mud almost knee deep, the troops wended their way down Sewell's rugged side, halting every few rods till some broken down wagon was turned over out of the way and set on fire...Among the property uselessly destroyed were the mess chests belonging to several company officers, containing all their provisions, and many valuable official books & etc."[3]

Confederate pickets heard and reported the noise from Rosecrans' camp during the night, but it was dismissed as nothing unusual. Maj. Isaac Smith recorded the event in his diary: "At one oclock that night I set out alone to visit the pickets, and found that one of the pickets had heard great rumblings of wagons but thought there was nothing unusual as they had heard them nearly every night. The camp was surprised next morning when daylight showed the opposite hill perfectly bare which had been filled with tents and moving men the day before...The general afterwards said "I should have advanced the pickets and felt the enemy; just think if I had known that was the way to manage the matter, I should have been the first man to occupy the enemy's camp, but live and learn."[4]

Sneaking off into the night did not seem the honorable thing to do to some of Rosecran's men. Others did not mind and welcomed any move away from Sewell Mountain. One Federal soldier complained that "This retreating is some-what inconvenient for the enjoyment of this rural scenery and for mental cogitations upon the possibility of our army's advancement to Richmond..." He went on to say that they had spent the day after their retreat foraging, and had got up "...all the beef and eggs for miles around us," and that he wanted "...a man servant, and wish you to send him immediately if you can. He must be an honest, industrious and strong colored gentleman, for otherwise he and I would not agree very well."[5]

Another Union soldier was so happy to leave the wilderness, that he celebrated by taking a bath. He wrote his wife saying, "I feel so elated that I have actually gone to the trouble of bathing from head to foot and putting on clean clothes throughout. A thing I have not done for some time."[6]

In their retreat, the Yankees destroyed a vast amount of material so as to expedite their withdrawal. Gen. Henry Benham wrote an account of these events in 1873: "The retreat of the rear guard of our command partook more of the character of a rout, than the ordinary retreat of unfought, unbeaten troops. I was told of a large destruction of provisions as they came down the mountain...whole wagon loads of beef and pork were tipped over in the deep valleys...and the men walked ankle deep, in flour from the stoved barrels, for a hundred yards together. $30,000 worth of stores were lost or destroyed."[7]

A member of the 42nd Virginia Infantry was among those who examined the position that Rosecrans had held. He found at the scene, "...a quantity of cooking utensils, chairs, tables, etc. (which I supose they had taked from the secessionists) a quantity of provisions and medicines which they had taken good care to render serviceless, and lastly though not least one rickety wagon and two horse frames upon which the buzzards anticipated a comfortable perch." Other witnesses also claimed that they captured two Yankee prisoners who had been too sick to move.[8]

General Lee drafted a new plan of advance on the very day of Rosecrans's retreat. The promptness with which he fashioned this plan demonstrated a greater facility than he had thus far exhibited in coordinating subordinates to execute his plans. Lee now wanted to move Floyd to the south side of the Kanawha River and have him advance to a point where he could cut the communications of the enemy on the Gauley. Lee would then attack the enemy, and with Floyd's help, drive them out of the Kanawha Valley.

Before the Rebels could advance, the roads had to be repaired so as to assure the transportation of supplies to their army. The road from Lewisburg to Sewell was in extremely poor condition and Lee's attention focused on necessary repairs. The portion of the road west of Sewell Creek, in present-day Rainelle, was repaired by troops of Gens. Loring and Floyd. The road east of Sewell Creek was repaired by the militia of General Chapman. The troops drained the road thoroughly, opened the waterways, and laid timber over all the soft and muddy portions, to form a flooring.[9]

With the Yankees no longer threatening and the turnpike repaired, General Lee allowed the 1,500-man militia under General

Chapman to be disbanded. Lee told the men they could go home to work their crops, but would be called out again if needed.

Lee's plan to advance General Floyd to the Kanawha River did not set well with Col. Henry Heth, of the 45th Virginia Infantry: "I had a long talk with General Lee and expressed to him my views as to Floyd's ability to exercise an independent command. I told him if Floyd was given an independent command it would be merely a question of time when it would be captured; that I did not think the Confederacy could afford to lose three or four thousand men, simply to gratify the ambition of a politician who was incapable of taking care of his men or fighting them, as a baby...I have seen too much incompetency in General Floyd to change my views."[10]

Actually, though Floyd was a "political general" Colonel Heth may have been too harsh in his criticism. His remarks certainly did nothing to dissuade General Lee from his plan. Floyd had proven himself good on the battlefield, with the fight at Carnifex Ferry; and had already shown considerable administrative skill. True, he was not a soldier by training, but Lee must have seen a level of competence in him sufficient to warrant confidence.

As the Union army retreated toward the Kanawha Valley, General Cox halted the brigade at Camp Lookout, or Spy Rock, some 12 miles west of their former encampment. Once there it was necessary to use the majority of their wagons for the transport of the sick. General Cox reported 426 men sick at Camp Lookout on Oct. 7.[11]

The necessity of foraging kept parties of men away from camp much of the time. One such party was attacked by Rebel cavalry near Lookout on the 7th, with no casualties, though seven soldiers of the 2nd Kentucky Infantry (US) lost their knapsacks. Feeling somewhat exposed at Lookout, Cox determined on the 7th to fall back on Mountain Cove and Hawks Nest, near Gauley Bridge. This movement was accomplished in stages over a two-day period.

Rutherford Hayes was among the Union men who had been happy to fall back on Gauley Bridge, but he could not confess to his wife that they had withdrawn without a fight. Instead, he lied to her, in saying that the enemy had retreated first: "Our campaign is

94

closed. No more fighting in this region unless the enemy attack, which they will not do...The enemy and ourselves left the mountains about the same time; the enemy first, and for the same reason, vis., impossibility of getting supplies...Our withdrawl was our first experience in backward movement. We all approved it. The march was a severe one."[12]

The Confederates had been unable to vigorously pursue the Yankees because of the poor condition of their horses and lack of provisions. Heavy rains had resumed on the 6th, and the following day Lee penned a letter to his wife, who was then at Hot Springs, Virginia. In the letter Lee's frustration is obvious:

Sewell's Mountain, October 7, 1861

I received dear Mary, your letter by Dr. Quintard, with the cotton socks. ...At the time of their reception the enemy was threatening an attack, which was continued until Saturday night, when under cover of darkness he suddenly withdrew...If I thought our enemies would not make a vigorous move against Richmond, I would recommend to rent a house there. But under the circumstances I would not feel as if you were permanently located if there. I am ignorant where I shall be. In the field somewhere I suspect, so I have little hope of being with you...The weather is almost as bad here as in the mountains I left. There was a drenching rain yesterday, and as I left my overcoat in camp I was wet from head to foot. It has been raining ever since and is now coming down with a will. But I have my clothes out on the bushes and they will be washed. The force of the enemy...is put down from 17,000 to 20,000. Some went as high as 22,000. General Floyd thinks 18,000. I do not think it exceeds 9,000 or 10,000, though it exceeds ours. I wish he had attacked us, as I believe he would have been repulsed with great loss...The rumbling of his wheels, etc., was heard by our pickets, but as that was customary at night in the moving and placing of his canon, the officer...paid no particular attention to it, supposing it to be preparation for attack in the morning. When day appeared, the bird had flown, and the misfortune was that the reduced condition of our horses for want of provender, exposure to cold rains in these mountains, and want of provisions for the men, prevented the vigorous pursuit and following up that was proper. We can only get up provision from day to day, which paralyses our operations.

I am sorry, as you say, that the movements of the armies cannot keep pace with the expectations of the editors of the papers. I know they can regulate matters satisfactorily to themselves on paper. I wish they could do so in the field...I hope something will be done to please them...

Always yours
R.E. Lee[13]

The following day General Chapman sent Lee a list of supplies which he had determined would be available to Lee from the counties of Monroe, Giles and Mercer. Chapman stated that with the proper transportation, a "safe and sure" estimate of supplies available would include 100,000 bushels of corn meal, 10,000 bushels of oats, 10,000 barrels of flour and 400,000 pounds of pork. He told Lee that if the Raleigh Courthouse (Beckley) was used as a general depot, there should be five points for collecting supplies: "County of Monroe - Cooks Mill 50 miles from Raleigh CH, Peterstown 48 miles distant - Red Sulphur 42 miles - Mouth of Indian 36 miles - & Packs Ferry 24 miles - Giles CH to Raleigh is 57 miles and from Monroe CH to Raleigh CH 39 miles...any amount of supplies needed could be obtained at the Dublin Depot on the Virginia and Tennessee RR drawn from east and west. This depot is located 20 miles from Giles CH and 77 miles from the Raleigh CH, whilst the distance from Jackson River Depot to Big Sewell Mountain, is 67 miles."

Lee also heard from Dr. O.A. Krenshaw, medical director of the Floyd and Wise brigades, at White Sulphur Springs: "Your communication requesting me to make preparation for the sick of Genl Lorings command is received. We have now more than one thousand sick of Genls Floyd and Wises Brigades and all available room is now overcrowded & an aggravation in the intensity of disease & increased mortality the consequence. I have taken the large hotel but it cannot be occupied until resting stones are put into it...I have taken all the building here except the highly finished & expensive or new rental cottages & if more sick are sent I shall be compelled to take them... The hotel is prepared the lower floor will contain 500 patients - the upper floor about 600 but there is an objection to using the upper floor from danger of fire..."

Of course disease and supply problems were not unique to the Confederates, and as General Rosecrans assembled his army in the vicinity of Gauley Bridge, he was again criticized in some Northern newspapers. His retreat from Sewell Mountain was generally perceived as premature and foolish. One writer claimed the entire affair was "one of the most foolish, as well as one of the most flattened-out expeditions that could possibly happen to an army...This flight will not be easily forgotten...if I mistake not, it was all caused by the inactivity and blundering of General Cox, and a few others of the same ilk. ...When our army came within ten miles of Camp Sewell, the roads were almost impassable...wagons and ambulances were broken to atoms. To a cosmopolitan journalist, the menacing attitude of both armies would indeed be a glorious sight. There stood the Southern troops on Sewell, giant-like in form, while our troops stood looking on with amazement, full of chagrin and disappointment."[14]

Yet another newspaper expounded upon the large numbers of sick soldiers in Rosecran's command: "Only six thousand troops are able to perform active duty...Between Gauley Bridge and Camp Lookout there are 1,640 patients in the hospitals, prostrated with camp fever (typhoid). At Cross Lanes near Carnifex Ferry, are 160 patients. Those that can bear moving are to be brought here (Cincinnati) as rapidly as steamers can be resumed. During the past two weeks there have been continuous rains...the campaign in Western Virginia is virtually ended...The enemy have already gone in the direction of Cumberland Gap."[15]

The Confederates were, of course, still encamped at Sewell Mountain and vicinity. Within a few days General Floyd's brigade would appear opposite Gauley Bridge, upon another mountain known as Cotton Hill; many miles east of the Cumberland Gap.

The next three days were spent by the Rebels repairing the road and accumulating supplies. General Lee's plan to advance Floyd's army into the Kanawha Valley was implemented on Oct. 12. This movement toward Gauley Bridge signaled the end of the Sewell Mountain campaign, as most military activities now focused on the eastern end of the great Kanawha Valley. A member of the 51st Virginia Infantry recalled the troops "...left camp about 9 o'clock our regiment in rear...transportation very insufficient, lack of ambulances to carry the sick & consequent neglect and discomfort..."[16]

Joseph Brown, of the 22nd Virginia Infantry, wrote that as the forces of Floyd and Wise departed Camp Defiance, they "...passed me lying on a small piece of oilcloth equipped with nothing but my tattered clothing, an official surgeons certificate testifying to a partial paralysis of the entire left side of my body, produced by lying in the puddles of water...There was a solemn stillness and a sense of lonliness to me, the abondoned soldier, which is to difficult to describe...A chattering squirrel in a chestnut tree nearby enhanced the scenery. The mountain songsters opened their orchestra in the trees, and as the sunshine warmed me into a sense of activity, I began an attempt to leave this lonely and deserted place. Slowly and painfully I dragged myself out to the turnpike that crossed the mountains on to my Lewisburg goal."[17]

Though Floyd's men had grown tired of camp life, not all were glad to leave the security of their entrenched position. The editor of the <u>Lynchburg Republican</u>, who was a member of Floyd's staff, described their departure: "We felt sad in leaving our entrenched position on Sewell, where we expected our little army to have covered itself again with the laurels of a glorious victory. But it may be that our work has been in vain, as the continually changing tide of war may yet float us back to them, and make them of great importance in our defense. They cover a space of about four miles, and though temporary in their character, were never less than formidable...It was from this point, they may exclaim, that the tide of Northern aggression was turned back in the war of our independence in 1861."[18]

General Lee was left at Sewell Mountain with approximately 4,000 troops. These consisted of the Tennessee regiments and the 14th North Carolina, along with Loring's men and parts of the Wise Legion, including artillery. That evening Lee ordered the Tennessee troops to occupy the eastern base of the mountain, some three or four miles from Lee's main camp. This movement was welcomed by the Tennessee soldiers as they suffered additional hardships from the frequent blowing of cold winds across the crest of Sewell Mountain. Once in their new camp some of the men slipped away in search of food, as described by Carroll Clark, of Company I, 16th Tennessee Infantry: "That night, a few of us decided to slip through the guard line, and get some potato pumpkins...we cut sticks about four feet long and sharpened each end...We found plenty of pumpkins in a field, stuck a pumpkin on each end of the stick, then shouldered the sticks and started for camp...I was the last one to cross the fence, and a few steps further, someone in the bushes yelled out, `Oh, yes damn you, we've got you.' The boys in front of me moved on in a hurry and I was in a loap when off fell one of my pumpkins, and of course down went the other, but I never halted, but pulled for camp. I supposed the fellow who scared me was the owner of the field, but next day I found out that it was some of our own men, out foraging, and decided to have some fun, and they had it."[19]

When the Tennesseans were separated from the Virginians under Loring, a soldier with the 42nd Virginia Infantry told his mother that he was not sorry to part with them. He said that "While they would unquestionably fight bravely an efficiently upon the field, they have all summer been very insubordinate and have been guilty of a great deal of very objectionable conduct - appropriating hogs, cattle, sheep, and fruit. Upon our marches and in the vicinity of our camps they have often stripped orchards and gardens...I do not pretend to say the Tennesseans have been the only offenders, for that is not so, but they have been the chief offenders." [20]

General Lee busied himself in organizing things at Camp Defiance and caring for the sick who had not yet been transferred to one of the military hospitals. From a surgeons report of Oct. 12, 1861, we can see that there were in camp 173 sick men remaining:

Returns of the sick men in Floyd's Brigade - Camp Defiance:

50th & 51st Regts. Va. & Guys Artillery sent to hospital -	39
42nd Regt. Va.	- 13
13th Georgia Regt. (7 very sick)	- 12
Mississippi Regt.	- 107
14th Regt. N.C. Vols. (26 sent to hospital)	- 80
	251
Sent to the hospital this day	- 78
Remaining	173

Respectfully Submitted

Wm. J. Clark[21]
Col. 14th NCV

The Lee Tree about 1928. Under this sugar maple tree General Lee pitched his tent in September 1861. It was here that Lee first saw the horse which he would later purchase and name Traveller. This tree stood until 1936. COURTESY FLOYD McCLUNG

View from Lee's HQ camp to his left flank, a hill known as Busters Knob. This hill was fortified by the 13th Georgia Infantry during the Sewell Mountain campaign. This is a 1928 view. COURTESY FLOYD McCLUNG

Area occupied as the main Sewell Mountain headquarters camp of Gen. Robert E. Lee in 1861. The rise in the foreground is a trench dug by Lee's army. COURTESY DAVID MILES, CHARMCO, WV

1990 view of the narrow ridge road which cuts through the wilderness between the Confederate camp sites. The scene must have appeared very similar in 1861. AUTHOR'S COLLECTION

SEWELL
(EARLY
James River and Kanawha Turnpike
Col. Samuel Lewis 1849
Col. W. H. Jones 1859
Col. George Alderson 1850
D. W. Blume
Withrow Mill
Alderson Mill
Landon Tully 1859
J. L. Blume 1865
Wm. Smith 1836
Jesse Thomas 1840
Samuel Henry 1830
Jesse Miller 1836
Dr. John Cooper — 1846 —
Shelton
Creek
Keeneys
Winona
A. J. Withrow Mill
Old Turnpike Road
Brackens
Bowyer
Chas. Masters
Washington Carver Camp
Joseph Baber
A. Middleburg
Richard Peters
George Baber
Sam T
New River
Lemul Rogers 1852
Jacob Rule 1850
Lemul Rogers 1859
Bowyers Coopers Boones
Fayetteville
Foot Trail
Manns
Babcock State Park Office
Bowyer Ferry
Sewell
Ledona — Rupert 1870
R. A. Flanagan 1846
Coop
George Hughart 1825
John Scott 1855
Joseph Davis 1840
Richard Tyree 1814

MOUNTAIN
(SETTLERS)

CREEK

45   38   33

MILE TREE FROM LEWISBURG

ROAD

SHELTON SCHOOL

OLIVER TAYLOR
1843

HUGH FERRY
1830
ALTHAR
CARAWAY
McGARY
DOUGLAS

GEORGE MASTERS
1839

HUDSON CAMPBELL

JAMES DEAL
1853

J. DEEM
1831
WALKER

STAGE

W. F. DICKERSON JOHN B. KEENEY

HENRY AMICK

JOS. KEENEY
1950

S. MABEL
1855

GEORGE PEIRCY
1844

ROAD

RICHARD F. TYREE
1824

STERGEON
1845

CLIFFORD
1885

PETER ANDERSON
1848

CATHERINE COOPER
1872

WRIGHT

ANDERSONS MILL
1848

TYREE MILL - 1824
AMICKS MILL
WALKERS MILL

E. DOUGLAS

CREEK

ISAAC GILKERSON

1835
1858
1883

WM. GILKERSON

MANNS CREEK

OLD STATE ROAD 1786

W. T. Lanners
203 Winchester
Fayetteville W. V. 25840

1990 view of the ridge road leading from Lee's Tree to the heights of his headquarters camp.
AUTHOR'S COLLECTION

1990 view of some trench remains at Sewell Mountain.
AUTHOR'S COLLECTION

The Campaign Abandoned

Floyd's march toward the Kanawha Valley progressed very slowly due to the poor roads and lack of sufficient supplies. Capt. B.S. Thompson, assistant quartermaster of Floyd's Brigade, was ordered into Monroe, Mercer, Giles and Pulaski counties, in search of provisions. General Floyd authorized Thompson to impress supplies and transportation, if he could not purchase them. He also kept parties of men out repairing the roads from dawn to dusk and ordered his regimental commanders to keep the soldiers from "prowling about over the country," and ordered that "no soldier be allowed to enter the houses along the road, or in any section of country the army may pass through." Lt. Col. Albert Gallatin Jenkins was kept busy scouting the numerous side-roads and passes along the route, and was later ordered to establish a line of express between the Kanawha Valley and Newburn, VA, on the East Tennessee and Virginia Railroad. Two Confederate cavalrymen were to be stationed at intervals of 10 miles each.

General Lee had initially hoped to join Floyd near Gauley Bridge and defeat the enemy. However, within three days of Floyd's departure, Lee had changed his mind. The reasons for this change of heart are several in number. Their combined forces had been seriously reduced by disease. The inclement weather persisted, keeping the roads in a frightful condition. General Loring had begun to ask Lee for permission to return to his line of operations in the east, where Loring's Army of the Northwest awaited him. The military hospitals in the area were already crowded to over-flowing.

Lee also found it nearly impossible to supply his remaining troops at Sewell Mountain, and he realized that to advance another 32 miles over the sodden turnpike would very possibly ruin his already precarious system of supply. Lee had working between Camp Defiance and the depot at Jacksons River, 54 wagons. This included eight hired teams hauling provisions between the depot and White Sulphur Springs, which was utilized as a supply terminal. Also 10 four-horse wagons and 26 two-horse wagons, hauling continuously between Sewell and the depot. These teamsters required 10 days travel from Lee's headquarters to Jacksons River, and six days from headquarters to White Sulphur Springs. A state of affairs certainly not conducive to active military operations. Lee also understood of course that the Yankees had very little supply trouble, with the Kanawha River spanning the distance from Rosecrans' headquarters near Gauley Bridge, to their well-stocked depot at Point Pleasant, on the Ohio River.

On Oct. 15, General Lee sent the 14th Regiment North Carolina Infantry, back to Meadow Bluff. That regiment had entered Virginia 750 strong just three months previously, and was now reduced by sickness to just 277 privates fit for duty. Also on the 15th, Lee wrote Floyd, saying that a spy of his had crossed into Rosecrans's camp at Gauley, using a pass issued him by General Rosecrans through his provost marshal, Maj. Joseph Darr Jr. The spy supplied Lee with detailed, though not precise information, as to the strength of the Federals; putting their number at 14,000. This estimate was actually almost twice their true strength.

Lee also explained to General Floyd why he had not yet assumed the offensive: "I should have advanced toward Gauley, had it been possible to take the road, with a view of harassing the enemy and damaging his retreat. I sent the quartermaster and commissary on the road to see what could be procured and they report literally nothing. I am obliged to send the North Carolina regiment back at once, their sick increasing..the men of the Wise Legion are suffering much for want of clothing. The horses of the command are without provender."

Lee also described the near desperate situation at his camp, saying, "We barely get bread from day to day. No forage." It was thus that General Lee's decision was made for him. He could march with few men and fewer supplies toward the Kanawha Valley, or he could assist the movement of provisions to General Floyd and focus his attention elsewhere. He chose the latter.[1]

The day after General Floyd received Lee's letter he wrote to the Confederate Secretary of War, advising him as to the condition of his command and his plans for winter quarters. He told the Secretary in part, that, "We remained (on Sewell) eleven days, and those days cost us more men, sick and dead, than the battle of Manassas Plains. Provisions were hauled up the mountain 16 miles from Meadow Bluff over the worst road in Virginia, and we were exposed to tempest of wind and rain; for the conformation of the ground is such that there are always storms on Sewell Mountain. Finally the enemy retired beyond Gauley..."[2]

Lee again wrote Floyd, on the 16th, advising him of what he knew about the locations and strength of the enemy. He also told Floyd that the occupation of Cotton Hill (a mountain opposite Gauley Bridge) would put his army in a position to annoy the enemy greatly. This was merely a suggestion as Lee left it to Floyd's discretion how best to deal with the Yankees: "You must judge of the means at your disposal how you can best operate against them or whether any aid can be given you on this side...General Loring thinks it important for his command to return to his line. The reports from there indicate another attack."[3]

That same day Lee issued orders for a military express to be established: "A military express will leave these Headquarters daily at 9 a.m. arriving at 3 p.m. Leave Lewisburg for Headquarters at 9 a.m. arriving at camp at 3 p.m. The express matter will be deposited at P.O. Lewisburg where the couriers will report daily at 9 a.m. A detail will be made of six mounted men to carry the military express between these Headquarters & Lewisburg; three running each way & one reporting daily at HQ at 8 a.m."[4]

While the Yankees were considerably better off than the Southern troops, disease remained a serious problem for them too. An officer with the 11th Ohio Infantry reported on Oct. 16 that his regiment numbered 717 altogether. But, sickness had reduced that number to just "2 Captains, 9 Lieutenants, and 281 non-commissioned officers and privates." This totaled only 292 men and officers, or a reduction by disease of 59%. Almost as tragic as the reduction of 63% experienced by General Lee's 14th North Carolina Infantry.

Another Confederate unit devastated by disease was the 20th Mississippi Infantry. One man wrote early in October that 50 Mississippians had died on Sewell Mountain. They had been there one week.[5]

On Oct. 17, General Cox wrote to his wife telling her about their rough experience at Sewell: "We had terribly rough weather at Sewell Mountain. Numbers of horses died from the exposure, and I feared many of the men would; but we came out better than we had reason to expect." He told her he had been well, except for his tendency to develop a head cold, which was worse when the "damp winds blow through the flap door of my tent or under the sides." And he said it was possible to keep warm at night by sleeping on a small cotton mattress, wrapped up inside "a pair of heavy woolen blankets, the fold at the bottom of the bed to keep my feet from getting out...the woolen quilt you made me doubled, then a heavy pair of blue woolen blankets, and if the night is very cold I pile on top of all this a heavy caped army overcoat in addition to my old grey overcoat, and sleep snug as a bug in a rug." As for the result of all their hardships, he wrote that "We marched to Sewell and marched back again. Gen. R. has been very severely criticized for the small accomplishment of the movement."[6]

The large numbers of sick troops who had been at Camp Defiance were almost entirely gone by Oct. 18. Lee had sent them to the hospitals at Lewisburg, White Sulphur Springs and Blue Sulphur Springs. On Oct. 20, Lee wrote Floyd, and for the first time specifically mentioned his plan to return to Richmond. He also made it clear to Floyd that he could no longer retain General Loring in this region: "I must inform you that General Loring has received dispatches tonight from Generals Jackson and Donelson confirmatory of several previous reports indicative of attacks on both their lines, and calling earnestly for aid. I have resisted these appeals for some time...in the hope of uniting in an attack with your force from the left bank of the Kanawha on General Rosecrans...I do not think it proper to retain General Loring any longer...and I have not heard what time you expect to make your contemplated movement down the Kanawha...and shall also send the Wise Legion to Meadow

110

Bluff...On reaching Meadow Bluff I will inform you of the probable time of my return to Richmond."[7]

The Yankees had reopened activity in the direction of the Staunton and Virginia Central Railroad, and it would have been improper for Lee to maintain such a large force in an area of inactivity. Lee issued marching orders to Loring during the evening of Oct. 20: "The dispatches from Generals Jackson (Henry R. not Thomas J. "Stonewall" Jackson) & Donelson which you this evening submitted to my inspection...endear me to direct your return with the portion of your command with you to your former station. You will therefore commence your march without unnecessary delay. I regret the necessity that calls you from this line at a time when the service of yourself & troops is important & take the occasion to thank you and them for the alacrity with which you came to it's support when threatened by an overwhelming force and the cheerfulness with which you have operated in its defense."[8]

The following day, Oct. 21, Lee and Loring departed Sewell Mountain, never to return. General Lee moved the soldiers remaining at Sewell to Meadow Bluff, establishing headquarters at the home of a local farmer named Deitz. At this same time General Floyd's forces reached Fayetteville after a march of 10 days. They were now within 10 or 11 miles of General Rosecrans. The Confederates found Fayetteville in a frightful condition, following a raid by the Yankees, as described by an unknown Confederate writer: "This whole town is devastated. The Yankees were here on the 19th, and burnt one store and set fire to several buildings, the Court House among them, all of which were extinguished by the inhabitants. They entered private residences and plundered and broke up every article of furniture, carrying off everything that could benefit themselves. I deeply sympathize with the people of this place. The few who are left are very kind to us, doing everything in their power to add to our comfort."[9]

Floyd's army continued it's advance, skirmishing with the enemy several times as they pressed westward along the turnpike. General Floyd established headquarters in a large two-story farm house, known as the Dickerson place. This was an excellent choice as it was near the junction of the Raleigh and Millers Ferry roads, off New River. In this position, Floyd could control all movements from across New River towards Fayetteville and other points south.

General Rosecrans was alarmed by the Confederate advance to Camp Dickerson, prompting him to hasten forward the work of clothing and paying his men, recruiting his teams and bringing back to the ranks the soldiers whom exposure had sent to the hospital. Rosecrans had received information which he believed reliable, stating that General Lee planned a move against him, while Floyd advanced along the south bank of the Kanawha River, catching the Yankees in a pincer movement. Believing that Floyd's appearance was a sign of this attack, Rosecrans remained quiet and expectant for several days, awaiting the development of events.

General Floyd began writing letters to the Confederate Secretary of War, and on Oct. 27 he sent a very curious correspondence to the Secretary: "I am now preparing batteries on the mountain side which will command the road along the river to the enemys camp, by which they receive supplies after they leave the steamboat...the enemy will perhaps cross and give me battle under the conditions which I demand for success. But if the enemy will not do so, his force is so powerful, and mine so small, that I shall be unable to do anything unless the Department can prevail on General Lee, to make a movement against his front....I have done my part of this work, but I have not heard of General Lee's movements..."[10]

Of course Floyd's claim that he had not heard of Lee's movements was false. Lee informed him on the 20th that he was sending Loring's army away and that he would move his camp to Meadow Bluff. It appears that General Floyd either forgot about Lee's correspondence or intentionally attempted to deceive the Secretary of War. Perhaps Floyd secretly felt that the opportunity of Confederate success in this region was past, and he wanted to shield himself from blame.

On Monday, Oct. 28, Lee received a letter from Floyd: "All my forces having arrived, I am now ready for active operations. I have cannon on the heights, commanding Montgomery's Ferry, and

112

I can cut the road up the Kanawha, by which alone the enemy receives his supplies....If you will now make a decided movement in advance with the army at Sewell Mountains, it is nearly certain that we will capture the whole of the Northern army, or drive it entirely from the valley."[11]

To this somewhat surprising letter from Floyd, General Lee responded that he advised Floyd on the 20th of Loring's return to the Huntersville line, that all the sick had been sent on to the various hospitals, that he would be leaving Meadow Bluff that day (the 29th) to visit the hospitals at Lewisburg and White Sulphur, and then proceed to Richmond. He explained further that Col. J. Lucius Davis was in command of the troops at Meadow Bluff.[12]

With this last dispatch to General Floyd, Robert E. Lee departed the Fayette-Greenbrier County area; he would not return during the course of the war. As was the case after the failure of his Cheat Mountain campaign in early September, Lee was much abused by the press for his lack of a decisive victory in western Virginia.

General Floyd remained in the area for two more weeks. He opened fire upon the Union army at and near Gauley Bridge on Nov. 1, resulting in an artillery duel of six days duration. The recent rains had caused the rivers to be swollen to such an extent that General Rosecrans was unable to put men across the river, and dislodge the Rebels, until Nov. 10. By Nov. 14, no Confederate forces remained in Fayette County. In the retreat General Floyd lost several dozen men, killed, wounded, or missing. Among those killed in action was Floyd's cavalry commander, Col. St. George Croghan. The retreat of Floyd's army continued until they reached the security of Dublin Depot, VA.

General Lee's aide, Col. Walter H. Taylor, described the situation as he and the general had left for Richmond: "...the lateness of the season and the condition of the roads precluded the idea of earnest aggressive operations, and the campaign in Western Virginia was virtually concluded...General Lee cannot be reasonably held accountable. Disaster had befallen the Confederate arms, and the worst had been accomplished, before he reached the theatre of operations; the Alleghanies then constituted the dividing line between the hostile forces, and in this network of mountains, sterile and rendered absolutely impracticable by a prolonged season of rain, nature had provided an insurmountable barrier."[13]

Lee's departure did indeed signal the loss of western Virginia to the Confederacy. Already, on Oct. 24, a majority had voted to establish a separate state, and West Virginia was forever lost to the Confederacy and the Old Dominion. General Lee reached Richmond on the afternoon of Oct. 31. At a later date Lee was asked by Gen. William E. Starke why he did not attack Rosecrans on Sewell Mountain. Lee responded that a battle would have been without substantial result, that the Confederates were 70 miles from their rail base, that the roads were almost impassable, that it would have been difficult to procure two days food, and that if he had attacked and beaten Rosecrans, he would have been compelled to retire because he could not provision his army. "But," said Starke, "your reputation was suffering, the press was denouncing you, your own state was losing confidence in you, and the army needed a victory to add to it's enthusiasm." Lee only smiled sadly: "I could not afford to sacrifice the lives of five or six hundred of my people to silence public clamor," he said. And there he left it.[14]

In an address before a memorial meeting at Richmond in 1870, former Confederate President Jefferson Davis had this to say about General Lee's western Virginia campaign: "He came back, carrying the heavy weight of defeat, and unappreciated by the people whom he served, for they could not know, as I knew, that, if his plans and orders had been carried out, the result would have been victory rather than retreat. You did not know it; for I should not have known it had he not breathed it in my ear only at my earnest request, and begging that nothing be said about it....Yet, through all this, with a magnanimity rarely equalled, he stood in silence, without defending himself or allowing others to defend him, for he was unwilling to offend anyone who was striking blows for the Confederacy."

114

Reenactors of the 26th Battalion and 36th Regiments Virginia Infantry at Sewell Mountain in 1989. A plaque was dedicated on Sept. 24, 1989, at the site of Lee's Sewell Mountain headquarters. AUTHOR'S COLLECTION

Plaque dedicated Sept. 24, 1989, at the site of General Lee's Sewell Mountain headquarters camp in 1861. COURTESY MELODY BRAGG

APPENDIX "A"

General R.E. Lee's War-Horse

Thomas L. Broun wrote from Charleston, WV, to the <u>Richmond</u> (VA) <u>Dispatch</u> of Aug. 10, 1886, in regard to Gen. Lee's war-horse, Traveller:

Traveler was raised by Mr. Johnson, near the Blue Sulphur Springs, in Greenbrier County, Va. (now West Virginia); was of the "Gray Eagle" stock and as a colt took the first premium under the name of "Jeff Davis" at the Lewisburg fairs for the years 1859 and 1860. He was four years old in the spring of 1861. When the Wise Legion was encamped on Sewell Mountains, opposing the advance of the Federal army under Rosecrans, in the fall of 1861, I was a major of the Third Regiment of Infantry in that legion, and my brother, Capt. Joseph M. Broun, was quarter-master of the same regiment. I authorized my brother to purchase a good, serviceable horse of the Greenbrier stock for our use during the war. After much inquiry and search, he came across the horse above mentioned, and I purchased him for $175 (good value) in the fall of 1861, of Capt. J.W. Johnson, son of the Mr. Johnson first above mentioned. When the Wise Legion was encamped about Meadow Bluff and Big Sewell Mountains I rode this horse, which was greatly admired in camp for his rapid and springy walk, his high spirit, cold carriage, and muscular strength. He neither needed whip nor spur, and would walk his five or six miles an hour over the rough mountain roads of Western Virginia with his rider sitting firmly in the saddle and holding him in check by a tight rein, such vim and eagerness did he manifest to go right ahead as he was mounted.

When Gen. Lee took command of the Wise Legion and Floyd Brigade, which were encamped at and near Sewell Mountains in the fall of 1861, he first saw this horse, and took a great fancy to it. He called it his colt, and said he would need it before the war was over. Whenever the General saw my brother on this horse he had something pleasant to say to him about "my colt" as he designated him.

As the winter approached, the climate in the West Virginia mountains caused Rosecrans' army to abandon its position on Big Sewell and retreat

117

westward. Gen. Lee was thereupon ordered to South Carolina. The third Regiment of the Wise Legion was subsequently detached from the army in Western Virginia and ordered to the South Carolina Coast, where it was known as the Sixtieth Virginia Regiment, under Col. Starke. Upon seeing my brother on this horse, near Pocotaligo, in South Carolina, Gen. Lee at once recognized the horse, and again inquired of him pleasantly about "his" colt. My brother then offered him the horse as a gift, which the General promptly declined, and at the same time remarked: "If you will willingly sell me the horse, I will gladly use it for a week or so, to learn its qualities." Thereupon my brother had the horse sent to Gen. Lee's stable. In about a month the horse was returned to my brother, with a note from Gen. Lee stating that the animal suited him, but that he could not longer use so valuable a horse in such times unless it were his own; that if he (my brother) would not sell, please to keep the horse, with many thanks. This was in February, 1862. At that time I was in Virginia on the sick list, from a long and severe attack of camp-fever, contracted in the campaign on Big Sewell Mountains. My brother wrote me of Gen. Lee's desire to have the horse, and asked me what he should do. I replied at once: "If he will not accept it, then sell it to him at what it cost me." He then sold the horse to Gen. Lee for $200 in currency, the sum of $25 having been added by Gen. Lee to the price I gave for the horse in September, 1861, to make up for the depreciation in our currency from September, 1861, to February, 1862.

In 1868 Gen. Lee wrote to my brother, stating that this horse had survived the war, was known as "Traveller" (spelling the word with a double "l," in good English style), and asking for its pedigree, which was obtained as above mentioned, and sent by my brother to Gen. Lee.

Lee and Traveller at Petersburg, Va. in 1864. This is a rarely published view of the general and his favorite war-horse. COURTESY WASH-INGTON & LEE

119

A seldom seen view of Lee and Traveller, taken in 1866. COURTESY WASHINGTON & LEE

Lee and Traveller from a turn-of-the-century painting. COURTESY WEST POINT MUSEUM

APPENDIX "B"

Rebuttal by General Wise

At about 8:30 o'clock a.m. September 9, I received a letter from General Floyd dated 1 o'clock a.m., announcing the advance upon him of the enemy from Sutton, and that they were within 12 miles of Summersville. He stated that his strength, including the regiment of Colonel McCausland, did not exceed 1,600 men, and called for the return of Colonel Tompkins' regiment, and for me at the same time to send one of my own regiments, saying that if I could not, I must call on General Chapman across New River for re-enforcements. This surprised me as to his forces. He brought out two regiments, little less than 1,200; was then joined by Colonel Wharton's regiment, 400; then by McCausland's and Tompkins' regiments, 800; making 2,400 men; and two additional regiments, one from North Carolina and one from Georgia, were within a day's march of him. At the time that I dispatched Colonel Tompkins to him, in my letter of September 9, addressed to General Floyd, I assigned unanswerable reasons why I could not send a regiment of the Legion. I was reduced by measles to a force of infantry and artillery of about 1,050 efficient men. It was very hazardous to remain where I was with this force. If one-third of it were taken away I could not prevent the enemy from approaching Carnifix Ferry by the Saturday road. I would have to fall back again to Dogwood Gap, lose all I had gained by driving the enemy beyond Big Creek, lose Miller's Ferry, and all opportunity of communicating with Generals Chapman and Beckley, and all the advantages of Likens', a first-class mill, to grind meal and flour for my men; but, above all, the governing reason was that I could not defend General Floyd's rear, if I had re-enforced him with my whole force and cross Carnifix Ferry. By his estimate he would have had but 2,700 men, and by my estimate, about 3,500, to have fought what I estimated at 6,000 and he at 9,000, in his front, with from 2,500 to 3,000 in our rear to cut off all retreat, and he was in intrenchments most unskillfully traced, behind works not worthy of Chinese. I begged him, therefore, to relieve me from the order to send him one of my fragments of regiments, and appealed to him to allow me to await further events and orders and the removal of the immediate pressure of the enemy upon me. The fact was, I had already twice fooled in going to Carnifix, and there was great danger in my falling back at all, with the probability of being ordered again to remain in camp.

But again, September 9, General Floyd addressed to me another dispatch, saying that the enemy at 5 o'clock p.m. of that day were advancing, about 4,000 strong, this side of Powell's Mountain; called upon me to hurry up Colonel Tompkins, and to send him at once 1,000 of my own men with one of my batteries. Again, September 9, in his dispatch No. 37, the enemy were advancing upon him through Webster under Rosecrans, and he ordered me to station my regiment for which he had sent at Dogwood Gap. Thus there was another perfect confusion of orders. No. 36 was received at 2:15 a.m. No. 37 at 2 p.m., September 10 (See the notes of verbal messages made by Mr. Lewis attached to dispatches 34 and 35.) I wrote to General Floyd September 10, 6:30 a.m., in answer to all these orders and dispatches, and at 10 a.m. I informed him that the enemy were advancing upon me. The same day he dispatched me his order No. 38, in which he reprimanded my delay, and ordered me to send him 1,000 infantry and one battery of artillery; he also required me to reply; state the hour of receiving this order and that of starting my reply. I was then within half a mile of the Hawks's Nest, mounted, directing the advance of my van-guard against the enemy. This order was received at five minutes past 12 o'clock, and at 12:30 o'clock, by his own messenger, Mr. Carr, I returned him my answer No. 38, dated September 10, telling him the hour at which his letter was received, that it found me meeting an advance of the enemy threatening my picket at the Hawk's Nest, and that all my force of three regiments of infantry, four companies of artillery, and two companies of cavalry were under arms, to prevent, if possible, the success of an obvious attempt to turn our right flank and to pass us up the turnpike, most probably to the Saturday road, to gain Carnifix Ferry in his rear. I should therefore exercise a sound discretion in obeying his orders or not.

At 12 or 1 o'clock at night, September 10 and 11, Mr. Carr and Major Glass returned with General Floyd's dispatch No. 39, dated September 10, 8 p.m. ordering me on the receipt of it to dispatch him all of my available force save one regiment, with which I would occupy my then position, unless I deemed it expedient to fall back to a more eligible one. He informed me that the enemy had attacked him in strong force; the battle had been raging for three hours - from 4 till 7 p.m.; that he still held his position, and thought the enemy would renew the attack by daylight in the morning with perhaps increased force.

Accordingly, the next morning I started to re-enforce him, and received verbal orders, when about half way to the ferry, to turn back to Dogwood Gap. General Floyd had given up his position, without the loss of a man, after fighting successfully for three hours, and in the act of being re-enforced by nearly my whole command, and by the two regiments from North Carolina and Georgia, in all reinforcements amounting to upwards of 2,000 men.

On September 11, at 7 o'clock p.m., I addressed to General Lee a letter, giving a report of General Floyd's retreat from Carnifix without loss of life or limb, but with considerable loss of public property.

On the same day I met General Floyd, just beyond Dogwood Gap, prostrate upon the ground, by the side of the turnpike. I rode up to him in the presence of several officers and asked him for orders. He replied that he did not know what orders to give. I had other conversation with him, particularly detailed in my last-mentioned letter to General Lee.

On the 12th September General Floyd issued several unimportant orders about guards and scouts, and about nightfall I received from him an invitation to a conference to determine upon a definite line of action. The result of the consultation was a retreat to the top of Big Sewell. Some unimportant correspondence occurred up to September 16, when myself and officers were called again to General Floyd's headquarters for consultation. As early as practicable, about 5 o'clock p.m., I went, accompanied by Major Tyler, Captain Stanard, Captain Wise, and Colonel Jackson. A memorandum of that conference will be found immediately following General Floyd's dispatch No. 45, addressed to me.

On the same evening, within half an hour after I left his camp, I was informed by him that it was determined to fall back again to the most defensible point between Meadow Bluff and Lewisburg; he would put his column in motion at once, and I would hold my command in readiness to bring up the rear.

On the 18th he inquired why I had not obeyed his order to fall back. On the same day, at 10:30 o'clock a.m. I replied that I had obeyed his order to the letter; that I had held my command in readiness to bring up his rear; that I considered the most impregnable position I then occupied as essential to protect his rear, and that neither the condition of the roads nor the health of my men would permit me to move them without great inhumanity to man and beast. In the next place, by moving back I would lose the command of Bowyer's Ferry and the old State road. I respectfully requested permission to remain where I was, as best obeying his orders. I refer the President and the Secretary of War to the report of my quartermaster, F.D. Cleary, to my letter of September 18, addressed to General Floyd, and to his of the 19th of September to me, respecting wagons and transportation, and to my letter to General Floyd of September 19, 11:30 o'clock p.m., about the policy of falling back.

On September 19, 2 o'clock a.m., I notified General Floyd of the advance of the enemy on my position. He replied by his letter from Meadow Bluff, dated September 19. I replied by my letter of September 19, 9:45 a.m. The only reply I received from him was his letter of September 22, ordering me to send him a piece of artillery, a 10-pounder gun manufactured on the Kanawha; this was instead of re-enforcements. I answered his call for the gun on September 23d; and that is the last letter which I have been obliged to write to General Floyd.

On the 21st of September General Lee addressed me a letter from the camp at Meadow Bluff. I replied to this on the 21st, at 5 o'clock p.m. (referring to his seeming reprimand of my failure to be united with General Floyd at Meadow Bluff), that I considered my force already united with General Floyd for the most effectual, co-operation; and I gave my reasons for his examining my position and determining between that and General Floyd's. He visited my camp, examined the ground, announced no conclusion upon the subject, but returned to General Floyd's camp.

On September 23 Major Tyler, under my instructions, addressed to General Lee two communications, announcing the approach of the enemy. On the same day General Lee addressed to me his letter of the 23d. On the same day I replied, announcing to him that the enemy were in strong force on top of Big Sewell. On the 24th he addressed me again. That day I advised him that the enemy were advancing upon me from Big Sewell, and at 7:30 o'clock a.m. I again addressed him in writing. On the same day he arrived at my position with a re-enforcement of four regiments. My advance guard had met that of the enemy on Monday, Tuesday, and Wednesday. By this time the enemy had received re-enforcements swelling their number probably to more than 6,000, and their scouts pushed close to our lines, occasioning frequent sharp skirmishes, in all of which our men and officers acquitted themselves to my entire satisfaction. Indeed, from the time that I first marched under General Floyd's orders until the moment of my recall my command was engaged, almost without intermission, in constant skirmishes, severely testing their courage, coolness, and endurance, and tending in a great degree to restrain the advance, embarrass the movements, and prevent the concentration of the enemy's forces. I am proud to say that every instance of attack and defense has only tended to increase my confidence in their efficiency.

At about 4:30 o'clock p.m. September 25 I received, while under fire on the field, the President's order to leave my command, transfer it to General Floyd and to report at Richmond with the least delay. After a moment's reflection, at 5 o'clock I addressed to General Lee my last letter to him, received his counsel, indorsed upon my note, advising me to obey the order with the least delay, and I left the camp, immediately - took time only to pack my baggage - started the next morning, and did not stop until I arrived at Richmond.

I have now made as full and detailed a report as it is possible for me to make in my present prostrated state of health. To recapitulate, then: In reply to General Floyd's report of September 12, of which he gave me no notice when he sent it to the Department, I aver that I did not fail to render him the best assistance in my power; that I defended his rear on this side of Carnifix Ferry; that had I obeyed his order and crossed the ferry, neither man nor beast of his command or mine would have escaped capture, wounds, imprisonment, or death. I aver the fact that he did not succeed so well in the construction of his temporary breastworks as he did in the defense of his rear. I aver that his intrenchment was not worthy of any command, either in site or construction, and that his facilities for retreat were wholly neglected and inadequate; that wantonly and unnecessarily he lost a large amount of public property, and would have lost all his artillery but for the good conduct and courage of Colonel Tompkins. I aver that if he ought to have crossed that ferry and remained in those intrenchments one hour to await the approach of a superior force of the enemy, and to fight the enemy for three hours without the loss of a single man killed, he ought to have waited another attack the next day and the re-enforcements that were marching to his relief. He estimates the enemy's force between eight and nine thousand, when they were not more than 6,000. Upon the close of the contest at night it was not, as he says it was, a mere question of time - it was impossible for him to discover whether it was a question of time merely - when he should be compelled to yield to the superiority of numbers. He had had plenty of time to have constructed his ferry and amply sufficient breastworks. He says, therefore, that he determined at once to recross the Gauley River and take position on the left bank, which he says he accomplished without the loss of a gun or any accident whatever. I aver that if he took position on the left bank of the Gauley he did not hold it, and ultimately - almost immediately - he left the left bank of the Gauley totally unprotected. Whether he lost a gun or not is yet to be ascertained. It is certainly credibly reported that he did lose one caison, 30,000 rounds of ammunition, a large amount of camp equipage and clothing, as well as supplies and provision, his own personal baggage and arms in part, and ninety-odd fat cattle, and that some of his pickets were cut off.

He says it was strange that his loss was only 20 men wounded. It is stranger still that he should have retreated with so few men wounded and

126

none killed. His men behaved with decided gallantry, and I have no doubt would proudly have stood the brunt of another day's contest. If he had crippled the enemy to such extent that they were in no condition to molest him in his passage across the river, he might well have stood the breast of their crippled forces in more than one bout. Nothing but extreme ignorance of the forces of the enemy and of the topography of the country could have engendered the belief that he could have beaten the enemy and marched directly to the valley of the Kanawha if he had been re-enforced before the close of the second day's conflict by General Wise's column and the North Carolina and Georgia regiments. General Wise's column and the North Carolina and Georgia regiments were moving up under his orders. Why did he not await a second day's conflict with the enemy? The necessity for his recrossing the river is not made plain, but contradicted by his own statement. He says he is confident that if he could have commanded the services of 5,000 men instead of 1,800, he could have opened the road directly into the valley of the Kanawha. Let me say that General Floyd is more efficient in commanding a force of 1,800 than one of 5,000 men. According to my estimate he had more than 1,800; he had 2,400 men; and as to opening the road directly into the valley of the Kanawha, that road is open already in a dozen places to any force, great or small. My cavalry, 240 strong only, had opened a road into the valley of the Kanawaha within 12 miles of Charleston, killing as many of the enemy as General Floyd's force did at Carnifix, and this on the 12th September, the very date of General Floyd's report. At any time that General Floyd will attempt to enter the Kanawha Valley in the way he proposed - by Twenty Mile, Bell's and Hughes' Creeks or the Gauley Bridge - General Rosecrans, if permitted, will open the road for him to enter it. He says:

> *This close correspondence shows distinctly enough the urgent necessity of so shaping the command in the valley of the Kanawha as to insure in the future that unity of action upon which alone can rest any hope of success in military matters.*

I aver that the hope of success in military matters ought not to rest on the command of General Floyd. I am not content that my command shall be transferred to him. I will confidently abide by my correspondence with him to show who ought to be the commander. If called upon to give advice to my superiors, I would say that General Floyd ought to be confined in his command to the Kentucky border, under some able superior, and that the command of the Department of the Kanawha ought to be given to Col. C.Q.

Tompkins, who is a soldier by education and natural qualifications, a gentleman, and a man who has an important stake in the country where he commands. He ought to be promoted to that command, with the rank of brigadier-general; and my Legion ought to be transferred to my immediate command somewhere in the East, leaving in the West such companies as prefer to remain there and allowing me the privilege to supply their place.

Whenever General Floyd shall think proper to take any other or further notice of these transactions, I will, if I think proper, take further notice of him. It is not so certain that the reasons which have induced him to take the course which he has will be correctly understood either by the President or by the Secretary of War. General Floyd selected no strong point in the mountain passes. On the contrary, he fell back from the mountains, dug a ditch in a meadow marsh covered by every hill around, and the breastworks of which the first rain covered over with a swelling flood. He cannot fight a superior force in any intrenchments that he has selected or constructed. General Lee is now in command, and his counsel had better be taken as to what policy ought to be pursued. I only ask that, if these explanations are not sufficient, I may have the opportunities of defense. If they are sufficient, I ask that my command may be transferred back to me, and that we be separated from the command of General Floyd. I refer to the accompanying charts of my positions at Camp Defiance and at Dogwood and to the map elucidating my explanations. I beg that, besides favoring this with your own attention, you will do me the kindness to bring this report and accompanying papers without delay to the immediate notice of the President.*

I have the honor to be, very respectfully, your obedient servant.

HENRY A. WISE
Brigadier-General

Hon. J.P. Benjamin, Secretary of War.

* Not Found

NOTE: This as an abridged version of Wise's statement from Richmond, after he had been relieved from duty at Camp Defiance. For the entire rebuttal see Official Records, Vol. 5, pgs. 150-165.

NOTES TO CHAPTER 1

1. United States War Department, <u>War of the Rebellion: A Compilation Of the Official Records of the Union and Confederate Armies</u>, 70 vols. in 128 books, (Washington: Government Printing Office, 1881-1901), Series 1, V. 5 p. 773.

2. B. Estvan, <u>War Pictures From The South</u>, (New York: D. Appleton & Co., 1863), p. 117.

3. Official Records, V. 5 p. 773.

4. S.A. Cunningham (ed.), <u>Confederate Veteran Magazine</u>, 1893-1932, 1917 p. 121.

5. Official Records, V. 5 p. 774.

6. Official Records, V. 51 pt. 2 p. 224.

7. Official Records, V. 5 p. 778.

8. Ibid., p. 774.

9. Ibid., p. 781.

10. Ibid., p. 784.

11. Ibid., p. 785.

12. Ibid., p. 785.

13. Ibid., p. 789.

14. Joshua Horton & Solomon Teverbaugh, <u>History of the 11th OVI</u>. (Dayton, Ohio: W.J. Shuey, 1866), p. 38.

15. Diary of A.B. Roler, Wise Legion, July-Sept. 1861, in the manuscript collections of the Virginia Historical Society, Richmond, VA.

16. "The Old Stone House," <u>West Virginia History Magazine</u>, Jan. 1971, p. 115.

17. Joseph A. Brown, <u>The Memoirs of a Confederate Soldier</u>, (Abindon, VA. The Forum Press 1940), p. 13.

18. Official Records, V. 51 pt. 2 p. 237.

19. Ibid., V. 5 p. 791.

20. Ibid., V. 5 p. 792.

21. Ibid., V. 5 p. 792.

22. Ibid., V. 5 p. 796.

23. Ibid., V. 5 p. 798.

24. Lawrence Wilson, <u>Itinerary of the 7th Ohio Volunteer Infantry 1861-64</u>, (New York & Washington: Neale Publishing Co., 1907), p. 61.

25. Horton & Teverbaugh, p. 41.

26. Official Records, V. 51 pt. 1 p. 448.

27. Ibid., V. 5 p. 156.

28. Ibid., p. 800.

29. Ibid., V. 51 pt. 2 p. 248.

30. Record book of Jacob D. Cox, May-Nov. 1861, Oberlin College, Oberlin, Ohio, p. 174.

31. Jacob D. Cox, <u>Military Reminiscences</u>, (New York, Charles Scribner & Sons, 1900), p. 98.

32. Terry Lowry, <u>September Blood</u>, <u>The Battle of Carnifex Ferry</u>, (Pictorial Histories Publishing Co., Chas., WV, 1985) p. 28.

33. Official Records, V. 5 p. 123.

34. Ibid., V. 51 pt. 2 p. 270.

NOTES TO CHAPTER 2

1. United States War Department, <u>War of the Rebellion</u>, <u>A Compilation of the Official Records of the Union and Confederate Armies</u>, 70 vols. in 128 books, (Washington: Government Printing Office, 1881-1901), Series 1, V. 51 pt. 1 p. 473.

2. Ibid., V. 5 p. 149-163.

3. Ibid., V. 5 p. 133.

4. From accounts found in the Lytle and Lowe scrapbooks, Dayton-Montgomery County Library, Dayton, Ohio.

5. Terry Lowry, <u>September Blood</u>, <u>The Battle of Carnifex Ferry</u>, (Pictorial Histories Publishing Co., Chas., WV., 1985), p.85

6. Papers of Capt. Robert W. Snead, Virginia Historical Society, Richmond, VA, letter of Sept. 10, 1861.

7. Official Records, V. 51 pt. 1 p. 41-42.

8. <u>September Blood</u>, p. 152-158.

9. Official Records, V. 5 p. 146.

10. Ibid., V. 5 p. 848.

11. Ibid., V. 5 p. 850.

12. National Archives, Record Group 109, Records of the Army of the Kanawha, Chap. 2, V. 94, General and Special Orders #73, Sept. 12, 1861.

13. Official Records, V. 5 p. 852.

14. Ibid., V. 5 p. 851-852.

15. Ibid., V. 51 pt. 2 p. 297.

16. Papers of Gen. Augustus A. Chapman, 19th Brigade Virginia Militia, in the manuscript collections of Duke University, Durham, NC, letter of Sept. 15, 1861.

17. Papers of Gen. Alfred Beckley, 27th Brigade Virginia Militia, in the manuscript collections of Duke University, Durham, NC.

18. National Archives, RG 109 Chapter 2 V. 94, General Orders #24, Sept. 15, 1861.

19. Ibid., Special Orders #79, Sept. 15, 1861.

20. Jacob D. Cox, <u>Military Reminiscences</u>, (New York, Charles Scribner & Sons, 1900), p. 109.

21. Official Records, V. 51 pt. 1 p. 481.

22. From the unpublished papers of Col. George Alderson, 1861, by courtesy of Mrs. Kenneth Swope, Lewisburg, WV.

23. Official Records, V. 51 pt. 2 p. 299.

24. RG 109 Ch. 2 V. 94, Special Orders #92, Sept. 16, 1861.

25. Official Records, V. 5 p. 853.

26. Ibid., V. 5 p. 854-55.

27. Henry Heth, (James L. Robertson Jr. editor), "Memoirs of Henry Heth," Civil War History, V. 8 #1 p. 15.

28. From papers of Lt. D.B. Baldwin, in the manuscript collections of the Virginia Historical Society, Richmond, VA, letter of Sept. 18, 1861.

29. Official Records, V. 51 pt. 1 p. 481.

30. Record book of Gen. Jacob D. Cox, May-Nov. 1861, Oberlin College, Oberlin, Ohio, p. 274.

31. Ibid., p. 276-281.

32. Ibid., p. 286-87.

33. From a letter published in the Richmond Enquirer, Oct. 1, 1861.

34. National Archives, Record Group 109, Records of the Army of the Kanawha, Chap. 2, V. 318, Letters sent by Gen. Henry A. Wise, letter of Sept. 18, 1861.

35. Official Records, V. 51 pt. 2 p. 302.

36. Cox records, p. 288-90.

37. Official Records, V. 5 p. 861-63.

38. Ibid., V. 5 p. 862.

39. Ibid., V. 5 p. 860-61.

40. Ibid., V. 5 p. 864.

41. From the unpublished papers of Col. Augustus Forsburg, 51st Virginia Infantry, in the manuscript collections of the West Virginia Archives, Charleston, WV.

42. From the unpublished diary of William Clark Reynolds, 22nd Virginia Infantry, in the manuscript collections of the West Virginia State Archives, Charleston, WV.

NOTES TO CHAPTER 3

1. United States War Department, War of the Rebellion, A Compilation of the Official Records on the Union and the Confederate Armies, 70 vols. in 128 books, (Washington: Government Printing Office, 1881-1901), Series 1, V. 51 pt. 1 p. 484.

2. Ibid., V. 51 pt. 2 p. 304.

3. Ibid., V. 5 p. 868.

4. Ibid., V. 5 p. 868.

5. James H. Mays, Lee Mays, ed., Four Years For Old Virginia, (privately printed, 1972), p. 17.

6. From the unpublished diary of William Clark Reynolds, 22nd Virginia Infantry, in the manuscript collections of the West Virginia State Archives, Charleston, WV.

7. National Archives, Record Group 109, Records of the Army of the Kanawha, Cap. 2, V. 94, General and Special Orders, Special Order #114, Sept. 21, 1861.

8. G. Moxley Sorrel, <u>Recollections of a Confederate Staff Officer</u>, (New York, 1905), p. 75.

9. "General Lee on Sewell Mountain," from <u>The Southern Bivouac</u>, January 1883, Number 5, p. 182.

10. Official Records, V. 5 p. 162.

11. Ibid., V. 51 pt. 1 p. 486.

12. From the unpublished papers of Robert E. Lee, 1861, in the manuscript collections of the Virginia Historical Society, Richmond, VA, microfilm reel B55 - Mss31515b - letter of Sept. 23, 1861.

13. Official Records, V. 5 p. 874.

14. Ibid., V. 51 pt. 2 p. 309.

15. RG 109, Ch. 2 V. 94, Special Orders #132, Sept. 23, 1861.

16. Official Records, V. 5 p. 874.

17. Official Records, V. 5 p. 873-74.

18. Ibid., V. 5 p. 878.

19. Ibid., V. 5 p. 878-79.

20. Ibid., V. 51 pt. 1 p. 486.

21. Lee Papers, VMS, letter of Sept. 24, 1861.

22. Ibid., another letter of Sept. 24, 1861.

23. "A Virginian's Dilemma," The Civil War Diary of Isaac Noyes Smith, 22nd Virginia Infantry, Sept.-Nov. 1861, As printed in the <u>West Virginia History</u>, April 1966, p. 184.

24. RG 109, Ch. 2 V. 94, General Orders #27, Sept. 24, 1861.

25. <u>Southern Bivouac</u>, p. 182.

26. Smith Diary, p. 184.

27. Official Records, V. 51 pt. 1 p. 487.

28. Ibid.

29. Ibid., p. 487-88.

30. From the unpublished papers of Gen. Jacob D. Cox, in the manuscript collections of Oberlin College, Oberlin, Ohio. Cox letter of Sept. 25, 1861.

31. Rutherford B. Hayes, Charles R. Williams, ed., <u>Diary and Letters of Rutherford B. Hayes</u>, (Ohio State Archeological and Historical Society, 1922), p. 102.

32. Walter H. Taylor, <u>Four Years With General Lee</u>, (Indiana University Press, 1962 reprint), p. 33.

33. T.C. Marten, "Anecdotes of General R.E. Lee" as published in the <u>Southern Historical Society Papers</u>, V. 11 p. 519.

34. Douglas S. Freeman, <u>R.E. Lee</u>, (New York, 1934-35), V. 1 p. 591.

35. Burke Davis, <u>Gray Fox, Robert E. Lee and the Civil War</u>, (New York, The Fairfax Press, 1956), p. 50.

36. J. Ward, <u>12th Ohio Volunteer Infantry</u>, (Ripley, Ohio, 1864) p. 40-41.

37. Official Records, V. 51 pt. 2 p. 312.

38. Ibid., 51 pt. 1 p. 488.

39. Joshua Morten & Solomon Teverbaugh, <u>History of the 11th OVI</u>, (Dayton, Ohio, W.J. Shuey, 1866), p. 46.

40. Official Records, V. 5 p. 879.

41. Ibid.

42. Ibid., V. 51 pt. 2 p. 313.

43. National Archives, Record Group 109, Records of the Army of the Kanawha, Chapter 2, V. 323, orders sent by Gen. Henry A. Wise, Special Orders #234, Sept. 25, 1861.

NOTES TO CHAPTER 4

1. From a letter published in the <u>Scioto Gazette</u>, Chillicothe, Ohio, Oct. 15, 1861, letter of Sept. 26, 1861.

2. From the unpublished papers of Frank Jones, 13th Ohio Infantry, in the manuscript collections of the Cincinnati Historical Society, Cinc., Ohio.

3. Henry Heth, (James I. Robertson Jr. ed.), "Memoirs of Henry Heth," <u>Civil War History</u>, V. 8 #1 p. 16.

4. Charles T. Quintard, <u>Dr. Quintard, Chaplain C.S.A. and the Second Bishop of Tennessee</u>, (A.M. Nell, ed., Sewanee, TN, 1905) p. 32.

5. "A Virginian's Dilemma," The Civil War Diary of Isaac Noyes Smith, 22nd Virginia Infantry, Sept/Nov. 1861. As printed in <u>West Virginia History</u>, April 1966, p. 184.

6. National Archives, Record Group 109, Records of the Army of the Kanawha, Chap. 2 V. 94, General and Special Orders. Special Orders #148, Sept. 26, 1861.

7. J.M. Miller, <u>Recollections of a Pine Knot, Campaigns of West Virginia, Kentucky and Fort Donelson</u>, (Commonwealth Publishing Co., Greenwood, MS, 1899), p. 7.

8. R.E. Lee Jr., <u>Recollections and Letters of General Robert E. Lee</u>, (New York, 1904), p. 48-49.

9. Jacob Delson Cox, <u>Military Reminiscences</u>, (New York, Charles Scribner & Sons, 1900), p. 119.

10. United States War Department, <u>War of the Rebellion, A Compilation of the Official Records of the Union and Confederate Armies</u>, 70 vols. in 128 books, (Washington: Government Printing Office, 1881-1901), Series 1 V. 5 pt. 2 p. 318.

11. Ibid.

12. Ibid., p. 319.

13. "General Lee on Sewell Mountain," from <u>The Southern Bivouac</u>, January 1883, Number 5, p. 183.

14. Rutherford B. Hayes, Charles R. Williams, ed., <u>Diary and Letters of Rutherford B. Hayes,</u> (Ohio State Archeological and Historical Society, 1922), p. 103-103.

15. From the unpublished papers of Gen. Hugh B. Ewing, 30th OVI, in the collections of the Ohio Historical Society, Columbus, Ohio.

16. From the unpublished papers of Stanley Matthews, manuscript collections of the Cincinnati Historical Society, Cinc., Ohio, letter of Oct. 2, 1861.

17. Hayes, p. 104.

18. From the <u>Report of the Joint Committee on the Conduct of the War.</u>, testimony of Gen. W.S. Rosecrans. (Washington: Government Printing Office), 1865, p. 10.

19. Official Records, V. 51 pt. 2 p. 320.

20. J. Ward, <u>12th Ohio Volunteer Infantry</u>, (Ripley, Ohio, 1864), p. 39.

21. From the unpublished papers of Col. St. George Croghan, Floyd's Brigade, manuscript collections of Duke University, Durham, NC, letter of Sept. 28, 1861.

22. Walter M. Taylor, <u>Four Years With General Lee</u>, (Indiana University Press, reprint, 1962), p.35.

23. From the unpublished papers of Richard N. Hewitt, 42nd Virginia Infantry, manuscript collections of Duke University, Durham, NC.

NOTES TO CHAPTER 5

1. From the Memoirs of Leroy W. Cox, "Experiences of a Young Soldier in the Confederacy," unpublished personal narrative in the manuscript collections of the Virginia Historical Society.

2. Rutherford B. Hayes, Charles R. Williams, ed., <u>Diary and Letters of Rutherford B. Hayes,</u> (Ohio State Archeological and Historical Society, 1922), p. 103.

3. From a letter published in the <u>Wheeling Intelligencer</u>, Oct. 16, 1861.

4. From the personal diary of Gen. Hugh B. Ewing, 30th Ohio Infantry, in the manuscript collections of the Ohio Historical Society, Columbus, Ohio.

5. United States War Department, <u>War of the Rebellion, A Compilation of the Official Records of the Union and Confederate Armies</u>, 70 vols. in 128 books, (Washington: Government Printing Office, 1881-1901), Series 1, V. 51 pt. 2 p. 324.

6. Jacob D. Cox, <u>Military Reminiscences</u>, (New York, Charles Scribner & Sons, 1900), p. 120.

7. James J. Womack, Walter Womack, ed., <u>The Civil War Diary of Capt. J.J.</u>

Womack, (McMinnville, TN, Womack Printing Company, 1961), p. 19-20.

8. From an unsigned letter to the editor of the Nashville Union and American, Oct. 11, 1861. Original in the manuscript collections of the Tennessee State Archives, Nashville, TN.

9. Official Records, V. 51 pt. 2 p. 325-26.

10. From the unpublished papers of Robert E. Lee in the manuscript collections of the Virginia Historical Society, Richmond, Virginia. Microfilm reel B55 - Mss 31515b.

11. From the unpublished papers of Col. Henry Heth, in the manuscript collections of Duke University, Durham, NC.

12. From the unpublished papers of Richard N. Hewitt, 42nd Virginia Infantry, in the manuscript collections of Duke University, Durham, NC.

13. James J. Womack, p. 20

14. From a letter published in the Cincinnati Daily Enquirer, Oct. 1, 1861.

15. From "General Lee on Sewell Mountain," in The Southern Bivouac, Jan. 1883, #5, p. 185.

16. Over the years it has been variously reported that Lee had at Sewell Mountain from 12,000 to 25,000 troops. In actuality his command at no time exceeded 9,000 men fit for duty. Numerous historians have also recorded that General Loring brought 9,000 men to Sewell Mountain. Actually he brought about 3,000 including the Tennessee Brigade of General Anderson.

17. "A Virginian's Dilemma," The Civil War Diary of Isaac Noyes Smith, 22nd Virginia Infantry, Sept.-Nov. 1861. As printed in West Virginia History, April 1966, p. 188.

18. Reminiscences of W.H. Adams, 60th Virginia Infantry, as published in the Fayette Tribune, Fayetteville, WV, Sept. 24, 1924.

19. From the unpublished memoirs of W.S. Powell, 14th NC Infantry, in the Southern Historical Collection, University of North Carolina.

20. "Civil War Letters from the Kanawha Valley," West Virginia Heritage, V. 2 #41, Oct. 14, 1967. From original letters in the manuscript collections of the University of North Carolina Library.

21. From the unpublished papers of Robert E. Lee, 1862, Virginia Historical Society, Richmond, VA.

22. Rutherford Hayes, p. 104-05.

23. From the unpublished papers of the Ninth OVI, in the manuscript collections of the Cincinnati Historical Society, Cinc., Ohio. MSS 505 Box 1, Folder 7.

24. Lee papers, VA Historical Soc.

25. Marcus B. Toney, The Privations of a Private, (Nashville, TN, privately printed, 1905), p. 25.

26. "A Virginian's Dilemma," p. 188.

27. From a letter published in the Wheeling Intelligencer, Wheeling, WV, Oct. 16, 1861.

NOTES TO CHAPTER 6

1. From the unpublished memoirs of Leroy Cox, 46th Virginia Infantry, in the manuscript collections of the Virginia Society, Richmond, VA.

2. Jacob S. Cox, <u>Military Reminiscences,</u> (New York, Charles Scribner & Sons, 1900) p. 122-24.

3. Joshua Horton & Solomon Teverbaugh, <u>History of the 11th OVI,</u> (Dayton, Ohio, W.J. Shuey, 1866) p. 49.

4. "A Virginian's Dilemma," The Civil War Diary of Isaac Noyes Smith, 22nd Virginia Infantry, Sept.-Nov. 1861, as printed in <u>West Virginia History,</u> April 1966, p. 190.

5. From the unpublished papers of Frank Hones in the manuscript collections of the Cincinnati Historical Society.

6. From the unpublished papers of Stanley Matthews in the manuscript collections of the Cincinnati Historical Society.

7. National Archives, records of the Adjutant Generals Office, Record Group 94, microcopy publication M 1098, Roll #6. The post war papers of Gen. Henry Benham, 1873.

8. From the unpublished papers of William McCauley, 42nd Virginia Infantry, in the manuscript collections of the Roanoke Co. Historical Society, Roanoke, VA.

9. United States War Department, <u>War of the Rebellion: A Compilation of the Official Records of the Union and Confederate Armies,</u> 70 vols, in 128 books, (Washington: Government Printing Office, 1881-1901), V. 51 pt. 2, p. 335.

10. Henry Heth, (James I. Robertson Jr., ed.), "Memoirs of Henry Heth", <u>Civil War History,</u> V. 8 #1 p. 19.

11. Record book of Jacob D. Cox, May-Nov. 1861, Oberlin College, Oberlin, Ohio, p. 348.

12. Rutherford B. Hayes, (Charles R. Williams, ed.), <u>Diary and Letters of Rutherford B. Hayes,</u> (The Ohio State Archaeological and Historical Soc. 1922) V. 2, p. 108.

13. R.E. Lee Jr., <u>Recollections and Letters of General Robert E. Lee,</u> (New York, 1904), Lee's letter of Oct. 7, 1861.

14. From an article published in the <u>Wheeling Intelligencer,</u> (Wheeling, WV), Oct. 16, 1861.

15. From an article published in the <u>Cincinnati Enquirer,</u> (Cinc., Ohio) paper of Oct. 12, 1861.

16. From the unpublished memoirs of John Hunter, 51st Virginia Infantry, in the manuscript collections of the Museum of the Confederacy, Richmond, VA.

17. Joseph A. Brown, Samuel M. Austin, ed., <u>The Memoirs of a Confederate Soldier,</u> (Forum Press, Abingdon, VA, 1940) p. 14.

18. From a letter written by the editor of the <u>Lynchburg Republican,</u> Oct. 12,

1861. As published in the <u>Nashville Union and American</u>, Oct. 24, 1861.

19. From the unpublished diary of Carrol H. Clark, Co. I, 16th Tennessee Inf., in the manuscript collections of the Tennessee State Archives, Nashville, TN.

20. From the unpublished papers of Flemming Saunders, 42nd Virginia Infantry, in the manuscript collections of Duke University, Durham, NC.

21. From the unpublished papers of Robert E. Lee, 1861, in the manuscript collections of the Virginia Historical Society, Richmond, VA. Reel B55 Mss31515b.

NOTES TO CHAPTER 7

1. United States War Department, <u>War of the Rebellion A Compilation of the Official Records of the Union and Confederate Armies</u>, 70 vols. in 128 books, (Washington: Government Printing Office, 1881-1901) V. 51 pt. 2 p. 347.

2. Ibid., V. 5 p. 900-02.

3. Ibid., V. 51 pt. 2 p. 348-49.

4. From the unpublished papers of Robert E. Lee, 1861, in the manuscript collections of the Virginia Historical Society, Richmond, VA.

5. From the unpublished papers of Col. Thomas Garnett, 48th Virginia Infantry, in the manuscript collections of the Virginia State Library, Richmond, VA.

6. From the unpublished papers of Jacob D. Cox, in the manuscript collections of Oberlin College, Oberlin, Ohio.

7. Official Records, V. 5, p. 908-09.

8. Lee papers, VHS.

9. From an unsigned letter to the editor of the <u>Richmond Enquirer</u>, Oct. 31, 1861, as printed in the <u>Nashville Union and American</u>, Nov. 5, 1861.

10. Official Records, V. 5, p. 924.

11. Ibid., V. 51, pt. 2, p. 360.

12. Ibid., p. 361-62.

13. Walter H. Taylor, <u>Four Years With General Lee</u>, (Indiana University Press, 1962) p. 34-35.

14. A.L. Long, <u>Memoirs of Robert E. Lee</u>, (New York, 1886) p. 493-94.

BIBLIOGRAPHY

■ **Books**

Brown, Joseph A. The Memoirs of a Confederate Soldier, Abingdon, VA: The Forum Press, 1940.

Chapla, John. 42nd Virginia Infantry, Lynchburg, VA: H.E. Howard Publishing Co., 1983.

Civil War Centennial Commission of Tennessee. Tennesseans in the Civil War, 2 vols., Nashville, TN., 1964 - reprinted 1985.

Cohen, Stan. West Virginia Civil War Sites, Charleston, WV: Pictorial Histories Publishing Co., 1990.

Cox, Jacob D. Military Reminiscences, Nashville, TN 1893-1932. Reprints of the National Historical Society.

Cutchins, John A. A Famous Command: The Richmond Light Infantry Blues, Richmond: Garrett & Massie, 1934.

Davis, James A. 51st Virginia Infantry, Lynchburg, VA: H.E. Howard Publishing Co., 1984.

Dickinson, Jack L. 8th Virginia Cavalry, Lynchburg, VA: H.E. Howard Publishing Co., 1986.

Egan, Michael. The Flying Grey Haired Yank, Philadelphia: Hubbard Brothers, 1888.

Estvan, B. War Pictures From The South, New York: D. Appleton & Co., 1893.

Evans, Clement A. ed., Confederate History, 12 Volumes, Atlanta: Confederate Publishing Co., 1899.

Freeman, Douglas S. R.E. Lee, 2 volumes, New York: 1934-1935.

Hayes, Rutherford B. and Charles Williams, ed., Diary and Letters of Rutherford B. Hayes, The Ohio State Archeological and Historical Society, 1922.

Head, Thomas A. Campaigns and Battles of the 16th Regiment Tennessee Volunteers, Nashville: Cumberland Presbyterian Pub. House, 1885.

Horton, Joshua & Solomon Teverbaugh. History of the 11th OVI, Dayton, Ohio: W.J. Shuey, 1866.

Humphreys, Milton W. Military Operations 1861-1863 at Fayetteville, WV, privately printed, 1926.

Lamers, William A. The Edge of Glory: A Bibliography of General William S. Rosecrans, New York: Harcourt-Brace & World, 1961.

Lee, Robert E. Jr. Recollections and Letters of Gen. Robert E. Lee, New York: 1904.

Long, A.L. Memoirs of Roberts E. Lee, New York: 1886.

Lowry, Terry. September Blood:The Battle of Carnifex Ferry, Charleston,

WV: Pictorial Histories Publishing Co., 1985.

Mays, James H. and Lee Mays. ed., <u>Four Years For Old Virginia</u>, privately printed: 1972.

McKinney, Tim. <u>The Civil War in Fayette County West Virginia</u>, Charleston, WV: Pictorial Histories Publishing Co. 1988-89.

Meredith, Roy. <u>The Face of Robert E. Lee: In Life and in Legend</u>, New York: Fairfax Press, 1981.

Miller, J.M. <u>Recollections of a Pine Knot: Campaign of West Virginia, Kentucky and Fort Donelson</u>, Greenwood, Mississippi: Commonwealth Publishing Co., 1899.

Moore, George E. <u>A Banner in the Hills</u>, New York: Appleton-Century-Crofts, 1963.

Peters, J.T. & H.B. Carden. <u>History of Fayette Co. WVA</u>, Charleston, WV: Jarrett Printing Company, 1926.

Quintard, Charles T. <u>Dr. Quintard: Chaplain C.S.A. and Second Bishop of Tennessee</u>, Sewanee, TN: A.H. Noll, 1905.

Reid, Whitelaw. <u>Ohio In The War</u>, Cincinnati & New York: Moore & Baldwin, 1868.

Rice, Otis K. <u>A History of Greenbrier County WVA</u>, Parsons, WV: McClain Printing Company, 1986.

Richardson, Albert D. <u>The Secret Service: The Field, The Dungeon, and The Escape</u>, Hartford, CT: American Pub. Company, 1865.

Scott, William F. <u>Philander P. Lane: Colonel of Volunteers in the Civil War, 11th Ohio Infantry</u>, privately printed, 1920.

Sorrell, G.M. <u>Recollections of a Confederate Staff Officer</u>, New York: 1905.

Taylor, Walter H. and Dr. James I. Robertson Jr. ed., <u>Four Years With General Lee</u>, Indiana University Press, reprint, 1962.

Toney, Marcus B. <u>The Privations of a Private</u>, Nashville, TN: privately printed, 1905.

United States War Department. <u>Report of the Joint Committee on the Conduct of the War</u>, Washington: Government Printing Office, 1865.

United States War Department. <u>War of the Rebellion: A Compilation of the Official Records of the Union and Confederate Armies</u>, Washington: Government Printing Office, 1881-1901.

Ward, J.E.D. <u>12th Ohio Volunteer Infantry</u>, Ripley, Ohio: 1864.

Whittlesey, Charles. <u>War Memoranda: Cheat River to the Tennessee 1861-62</u>, Cleveland, Ohio: 1884.

Williams, T.H. <u>Hayes of the Twenty Third</u>, New York: Alfred A. Knopf, 1965.

Womack, Walter. ed., <u>The Civil War Diary of Captain J.J. Womack Co.E 16th. Tennessee Volunteers</u>, McMinnville, Tenn: Womack Printing Company, 1961.

▪ Magazines and Journals

Civil War History, "The Memoirs of Henry Heth," Vol. 8 #1 p. 13.
Confederate Veteran Magazine, (CVM) in order of date:
CVM, June 1898, p. 292, "Lee and Traveller" by Thomas L. Brown.
CVM, March 1899, p. 116-18, "Lee at Cheat Mtn" with Sewell Mtn included.
CVM, December 1907, p.548, "Trainer of Traveller - Frank Paige."
CVM, March 1917, p. 120-21, "In The Year 1861."
CVM, March 1922, p. 117, "General Lee on Traveller."
CVM, April 1930, p.142, "The Rending of Virginia."
CVM, April 1931, p. 141 "General John B. Floyd."
CVM, December 1932, p. 423, "Famous War Horses."
The Southern Bivouac, "General Lee on Sewell Mtn," January 1883 #5   p. 182.

Southern Historical Society Papers, "Anecdotes of General R.E. Lee," by T.C. Morton, Vol. 11, p. 519.

West Virginia Heritage, "Civil War Letters From The Kanawha Valley," Vol. 2, #41, Oct. 14, 1967.

West Virginia History Magazine (WVH) in order of date:
WVH, July 1944, "The Campaigns of McClellan and Rosecrans in West Virginia."
WVH, October 1944, "Jacob D. Cox in West Virginia."
WVH, April 1947, "General John B. Floyd and the West Virginia Campaign of 1861."
WVH, July 1953, "Fayetteville West Virginia During the Civil War."
WVH, April 1965, "Colonel George S. Patton and the 22nd Va. Inf."
WVH, April 1966, "A Virginians Dilemma," The Civil War Diary of Isaac N. Smith, 22nd Va. Inf., Sept.-Nov. 1861.
WVH, October 1969, "The Unfortunate Military Career of Henry A. Wise in West Virginia.

West Virginia Review (WVR) in order of date:
WVR, October 1925, "The Destruction of Gauley Bridge."
WVR, November 1930, "The Journal of a Soldier of 1862."
WVR, May 1934, "Albert Gallatin Jenkins, A Confederate Portrait."
WVR, September 1934, "Episode at Big Sewell."
WVR, October 1935, "After the Battle of Carnifex Ferry."
WVR, October 1946, "The Death of Col. St. George Croghan."

▪ Newspapers & Newspaper Articles

Charleston Gazette, Charleston, WV, Sept. 17, 1922, "Bahlman Gives History of Men Serving in '61."

Charleston Gazette, Jan. 10, 1926, "Civil War in the Kanawha Valley Saw Many Engagements."

Cincinnati Daily Enquirer, Cinn., Ohio, various items September and October 1861.

Fayette Tribune, Fayetteville, WV, Jan. 8, 1933, "Recollections of A.W. Hamilton.

Fayette Tribune, Sept. 24, 1924, "Reminiscences of W.H. Adams, 60th Virginia Infantry."

Nashville Union and American, Nashville, TN, various issues September and October 1861.

New York Herald, (NYH) and New York Times (NYT) in order of date:

NYH, Aug. 23, 1861, "Skirmish At The Hawk's Nest."

NYH, Aug. 29, 1861, "Important News From The Kanawha Valley."

NYH, Sept. 17, 1861, "Retreat Of The Rebels Wise & Floyd."

NYH, Oct. 4, 1861, "Reported Battle Between General Cox and the Rebels."

NYH, Oct. 7, 1861, "The Seat Of War In West Virginia."

NYH, Oct. 30, 1861, "Important News From West Virginia."

NYH, Nov. 8, 1861, "The Fighting At Gauley Bridge & Cotton Hill."

NYT, Nov. 10, 1861, "The Fighting Between Floyd And Rosecrans."

NYT, Nov. 23, 1861, "The Scene Of Floyd's Repulse."

Richmond Dispatch, Richmond, VA, various issues between August and October 1861.

Richmond Enquirer, Richmond, VA, various issues between September and October 1861.

Scioto Gazette, Chillicothe, Ohio, Oct. 15, 1861 and various issues between September and October 1861.

■ Manuscripts & Narratives

Papers of Col. George Alderson, 1861, courtesy of Mrs. Kenneth Swope, Lewisburg, WV.

Papers of Lt. D.B. Baldwin, in the manuscript collections of the Virginia Historical Society, Richmond, VA, (51st VA. Inf.).

Post war papers of Gen. Henry Benham, National Archives, RG 94 Microcopy M-1098, Roll #6.

Memoirs of Capt. Alexis Buster, 60th Virginia Infantry, courtesy of Dr. and Mrs. J.M. Laing, Lewisburg, WV.

Papers of Gen. A.A. Chapman, 19th Brigade Virginia Militia, in the manuscript collections of Duke University, Durham, NC.

Diary of Carroll Clark, 16th Tennessee Infantry, in the manuscript collections of the Tennessee State Archives, Nashville, TN.

Roy Bird Cook collection, various WV Civil War items in the manuscript collections of West Virginia University, Morgantown, WV.

Regimental record book of Gen. Jacob D. Cox, May-November 1861, manuscript collections of Oberlin College, Oberlin, Ohio.

Papers of Gen. Jacob D. Cox, memoirs and unpublished letters, 1861-65, manuscript collections of Oberlin College, Oberlin, OH.

Memoirs of Leroy Wesley Cox: Experiences of a Young Soldier in the Confederacy. Unpublished personal narrative, manuscript collections of the Virginia Historical Society, Richmond, VA.

Papers of Col. St. George Croghan, Wise Legion Cavalry - AKA - 10th Regt. Va. Cavalry, manuscript collections of Duke University, Durham, NC.

Papers of Gen. Hugh B. Ewing, 30th OVI, manuscript collections of the Ohio Historical Society, Columbus, OH.

Papers of Gen. John B. Floyd and the Army of the Kanawha, National Archives, Chap. 2, Vol. 94 and Chap. 2, Vol. 96, General and Special Orders, 1861, Record Group 109.

Papers of Col. Augustus Forsberg, 51st Virginia Infantry, manuscript collections of Washington and Lee University, Lexington, VA.

Letters from the 45th Virginia Infantry, manuscript collections of West Virginia University, Morgantown, WV.

Papers of Col. Thomas Garnett, 48th Virginia Infantry, manuscript collections of the Virginia State Library, Richmond, VA.

Papers of Col. Henry Heth, 45th Virginia Infantry, manuscript collection of Duke University, Durham, NC.

Papers of Richard N. Hewitt, 42nd Virginia Infantry, manuscript collections of Duke University, Durham, NC.

Diary of C.L. Howard, 13th Georgia Infantry, manuscript collections of the Georgia State Archives, Atlanta, GA.

Memoirs of John Hunter, 51st Virginia Infantry, manuscript collections of the Museum of the Confederacy, Richmond VA.

Papers of Frank Jones, 13th Ohio Volunteer Infantry, manuscript collections of the Cincinnati Historical Society, Cinn., OH.

Papers and official correspondence of Gen. Robert E. Lee, manuscript collections of the Virginia Historical Society, Richmond, VA.

Papers of Col. John W. Lowe, 12th Ohio Volunteer Infantry, Dayton-Montgomery County Public Library, Dayton, OH.

Diary of Arnold Moss Mason, 16th Tennessee Infantry, Sept. 6 to Dec. 28, 1861, manuscripts of the Tennessee State Archives, Nashville, TN.

Papers of Stanley Matthews, 23rd Ohio Volunteer Infantry, in the manuscript collection of the Cincinnati Historical Society.

Papers of William McCauley, 42nd Virginia Infantry, manuscript collections of the Roanoke Co. Historical Society, Roanoke VA.

Diary of Samuel J. Mullins, 42nd Virginia Infantry, copy in the possession of Mrs. Gravely, Martinsville, VA.

Papers and documents of the 9th Ohio Volunteer Infantry, manuscript collections of the Cincinnati Historical Society, Cincinnati, OH.

Papers of George S. Patton, 22nd Virginia Military Institute, Lexington, VA.

Pollock Papers, 14th North Carolina Infantry, Southern Historical Society Collection, University of North Carolina.

Papers of C.S. Powell, 14th North Carolina Infantry, S.H.S.C. University of North Carolina.

Diary of William Clark Reynolds, 22nd Virginia Infantry, manuscript collections of the West Virginia State Archives, Charleston, WV.

Diary of A.B. Roler, Wise Legion, July-September 1861, manuscript collections of the Virginia Historical Society, Richmond, VA.

Papers of Fleming Saunders, 42nd Virginia Infantry, manuscript collection.

"Diary of a Border Ranger," James D. Sedinger, 8th Virginia Cavalry, unpublished narrative, West Virginia State Archives, Charleston, WV.

Papers of Isaac Noyes Smith, 22nd Virginia Infantry, manuscript collections of the Virginia Historical Society, Richmond, VA.

Papers of Capt. Robert W. Snead, 50th Virginia Infantry, manuscript collections of the Virginia, Historical Society, Richmond, VA.

Diary of Andrew Stairwalt, 23rd Ohio Infantry, unpublished personal narrative in the manuscript collections of the Rutherford B. Hayes Center, Freemont, OH.

Papers of Gordon Thompson, 60th Virginia Infantry, courtesy of Roger Thompson, 130 W. 11th Ave. Huntington, WV.

Papers of R.D. VanDuerson, 12th Ohio Volunteer Infantry, manuscript collections of the Ohio Historical Society, Columbus OH.

Index

Note: Names of the most prominent personalities and the most frequently used place
names are not indexed in their entirety.

Phillips Ga. Legion - 21, 64, 68
Pocahontas Co., WV - 1, 46

Randolph Co., WV - 39, 52, 69
Richmond, VA - 5, 17, 21, 55, 81, 92, 110, 113
Rich Mountain, WV - 43, 59
Rosecrans, William S. - 7, 10, 17, 20, 24, 29, 37, 41, 45, 49, 54, 59, 63, 66, 77, 80, 84, 93, 97, 108, 112, 114

Schenck, Robert C. - 63
7th Ohio Infantry - 8, 10, 17, 21
60th Va. Infantry - 41, 47, 65, 67, 82
Smith, Isaac N. - 49, 82, 92
Spalding, James W. - 65-67
Spy Rock, WV - 25-26, 29, 32, 94
Staunton, VA - 81, 111
Summersville, WV - 17
Sunday Road - 7, 9, 21, 25, 32, 44

Taylor, Walter H. - 40, 51, 53, 68, 78, 113
Tennessee Infantry - 68, 78-79, 85, 99-100
10th Ohio Infantry - 18, 86
13th Ohio Infantry - 20, 61, 77
30th Ohio Infantry - 61, 65, 77
36th Va. Infantry - 24, 47, 62
12th Ohio Infantry - 19, 52, 67
28th Ohio Infantry - 20
22nd Va. Infantry - 17, 24, 33, 40, 46-47, 61, 98
27th Brigade Va. Militia - 2, 31, 34
26th Ohio Infantry - 61
26th Btn. Va. Infantry - 51
23rd Ohio Infantry - 20, 50, 61, 77, 84
Tyler, Erastus B. - 8, 21, 30, 42
Tyree, Frank - 5, 22

Valley Mountain, WV - 1, 8

White Sulphur Springs, WV - 1, 30, 61-63, 67, 97, 108, 110, 113
Wilderness Road - 23, 27, 43
Wise, Henry A. - 1, 5, 10, 17, 21, 27, 32, 39, 43, 47, 52, 55, 59, 67, 82, 98
Wise Legion - 4, 8, 11, 21, 28, 37, 43, 78, 81, 83, 97, 99, 110

A Note From the Author

Like cancer on the soul of the nation, the Civil War digested the national fabric as father turned against son, brother against brother, and even the heavens wept. Related here, for the first time, is the true story of an unfortunate campaign in that unfortunate war.

When a relatively unknown Robert E. Lee arrived in the wilds of western Virginia, America's Civil War odyssey, which would consume four years, was a mere four months old. We as a people had taken but a few steps on a long dark journey.

The Sewell Mountain range of Fayette County, Virginia, was of little note until the tide of war determined the areas strategic importance. Here, Robert E. Lee, a 54-year-old Virginia aristocrat and quintessential gentleman soldier, stood in defense of his native state. His opponent, William S. Rosecrans, was a 42-year-old Ohio native and warfare novice, having had no prior combat experience.

This then is the tale of a little-known campaign in a well-known war. This is the story of a time when there was pain in the American heart, and blood on the Laurel.

Tim McKinney
1990

The author on a 1989 relic hunt in WV.
COURTESY JERRY McKINNEY,
CARTHAGE, IN

Tim McKinney is a native of Fayette County, West Virginia, and is vice president of the Fayette County Historical Society. He is author of <u>The Civil War in Fayette County</u>, published in 1988. Mr. McKinney is employed by the Dept. of Safety at West Virginia Tech, Montgomery, WV. He can be contacted at Box 266, Charlton Heights, WV 25040.

148